WALKING CINCINNATI

Scenic Hikes Through The Parks & Neighborhoods
of Greater Cincinnati & Northern Kentucky

Second Edition

by Darcy & Robert Folzenlogen

WILLOW PRESS
Littleton, Colorado

ISBN: 0-9620685-5-1
Library of Congress Catalog Card Number: 93-61339

Published by **Willow Press**
      6053 S. Platte Canyon Rd.
      Littleton, Colorado 80123

Printed by Otto Zimmerman & Son Company, Inc.
      Newport, Kentucky

Typesetting by Debbie Lynn
      Mass Marketing Inc.
      Cincinnati, Ohio

Photos by Authors
Maps by Authors; many were adapted from those provided
  by Parks, Nature Preserves and Neighborhoods covered
  in this Guide.
Cover layout by Jan Jolley, Otto Zimmerman & Son Company, Inc.,
  Newport, Kentucky

For Sarah, Zach & Ally

ACKNOWLEDGEMENTS

Our sincere thanks to the many librarians, clerks, principals, secretaries and public relations personnel whose insight and assistance were instrumental in the production of this guide. Special thanks to the following persons for their generous contribution to our research:

Ms. Cindy Abell, Hughes High School
Ms. Teresa Brum, Historic Preservation Specialist, Newport, Kentucky
Mr. Charles Carey, Xavier University
Mr. Jim Farfsing, Coordinator of Outdoor Education, Cincinnati Recreation Commission
Ms. Mildred Hargreaves, Cincinnati Park Board
Ms. Anne Keller, Public Library of Cincinnati & Hamilton County
Ms. Karen Keown, Bellevue Historic Preservation Commission
Mr. Steve Kottsy, Milford Historical Society
Ms. Sabrina Nelson, Pleasant Ridge
Ms. Mary O'Driscoll, Montgomery Historical Society
Ms. Gayle Pille, Kenton County Conservation Board & Kentucky Trail Advisory Committee
Mr. Ellis Rawnsley, Terrace Park
Mr. Bill Thomas, Fort Thomas Tree Commission
Ms. Vivian Wagner, Cincinnati Park Board
Ms. Claire Young, University of Cincinnati
Mr. Ken Ziegel, Hyde Park Community United Methodist Church

We also wish to thank the staffs at Mass Marketing, Inc., and Otto Zimmerman & Son Company, Inc., for their creative and technical assistance.

Last but not least, our thanks to Sarah, Zach and Ally for their love, patience and moral support!

— *Darcy & Robert Folzenlogen*

CONTENTS

FOREWORD

With the publication of the first edition of **Walking Cincinnati,** in 1989, we set the goal of introducing residents and visitors to the cultural and natural history of our city, hoping that this knowledge would spawn an increased commitment to the protection and preservation of our historic landmarks and nature preserves. The response to that book has been most gratifying and we have thus produced this Second Edition which broadens the scope of the original guide.

Walking Cincinnati is a guide to over 80 hikes through the historic neighborhoods and nature preserves of Greater Cincinnati and Northern Kentucky. The walks represent fifty-nine areas across the Tristate, chosen to reflect the rich diversity of our region. Each walk is illustrated with a map and each hiking area is accompanied by a photo and narrative which portray the flavor and history of that location. Trail mileage, local terrain and directions to the area are provided for each walk.

Appendix I introduces readers to the natural and cultural history of Greater Cincinnati and Appendix II lists local conservation and preservation organizations that work to protect that heritage.

We hope that this guide will encourage residents and visitors to explore our parks and neighborhoods on foot. An increased awareness of our natural and cultural resources will most certainly prompt a greater commitment to their continued protection.

— Darcy & Robert Folzenlogen

LOCATION OF HIKING AREAS

1. Miami Whitewater Forest
2. Farbach-Werner Nature Preserve
3. Gilmore Ponds Preserve
4. Winton Woods
5. Glendale
6. Wyoming
7. Sharon Woods
8. Little Miami Scenic Trail
9. Montgomery Historic District
10. Seymour Nature Preserve
11. Caldwell Park
12. French Park
13. Pleasant Ridge
14. Mt. Airy Forest & Arboretum
15. LaBoiteaux Woods
16. Spring Grove Cemetery
17. Avon Woods Outdoor Education Center
18. Xavier University/Avondale
19. Hyde Park
20. Ault Park/Observatory Historic District
21. Mariemont
22. Terrace Park
23. Kelley Nature Preserve
24. Milford
25. Cincinnati Nature Center
26. The Oxbow
27. Shawnee Lookout Park
28. Mitchell Memorial Forest
29. Harrison Memorial/Congress Green
30. Sayler Park
31. Embshoff Woods & Nature Preserve
32. Mt. Echo Park
33. Clifton
34. University of Cincinnati
35. Fairview Park
36. Over-The-Rhine/Liberty Hill
37. Plum St./Central Parkway/Eighth St.
38. Skywalk/Fountain Square/Fifth St.
39. Cincinnati Riverfront/Lytle Park Historic District
40. Eden Park
41. Mt. Adams
42. Alms Park/Mt. Lookout/Tusculum
43. Lunken Airport
44. Magrish Riverlands Preserve
45. California Woods Nature Preserve
46. Stanbery Park
47. Withrow Nature Preserve
48. Woodland Mound Park
49. Boone County Cliffs State Nature Preserve
50. Doe Run Lake
51. Highland Cemetery Forest Preserve
52. Devou Park
53. West Covington/MainStrasse
54. Covington Riverside District & Suspension Bridge
55. Newport: Civic & Mansion Hill Districts
56. Newport's East Row Historic District
57. Bellevue/Dayton Levee Walk
58. Ft. Thomas Military Reservation/Tower Park
59. Fort Thomas Landmark Tree Trail

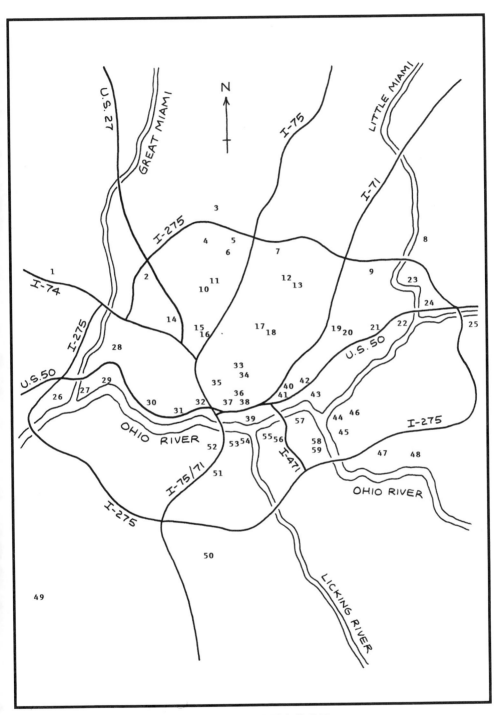

**HIKING AREAS OF
GREATER CINCINNATI & NORTHERN KENTUCKY**

TRAIL DATA

Hike	Mileage	Terrain
1. Miami Whitewater Forest		
Badlands Trail	1.75	hilly; steep areas
Oakleaf Trail	.75	hilly
Tallgrass Prairie Trail	.7	rolling
Parcours Fitness Trail	1.0	rolling
2. Farbach-Werner Nature Preserve		
Pin Oak Trail	.9	flat
3. Gilmore Ponds Preserve	1.5	flat
4. Winton Woods		
Hike/Bike Trail Loop	2.8	flat
Kingfisher Trail	1.1	rolling; few hills
Parcours Trail	1.0	hilly
West Fork Dam	.5-1.5	flat
5. Glendale	2.6	rolling
6. Wyoming	2.6	flat
7. Sharon Woods		
Gorge Trail	1.25	hilly; steep areas
Hike/Bike Trail	2.8	rolling
8. Little Miami Scenic Trail		
Loveland-Foster (roundtrip)	7.0	flat
Milford-Loveland (one way)	8.0	flat
Morrow-Ft. Ancient (one way)	5.0	flat
Ft. Ancient-Mather's Mill (roundtrip)	2.5	flat
9. Montgomery Historic District	2.0	flat
10. Seymour Nature Preserve	1.5	hilly
11. Caldwell Park	1.4-1.9	hilly; steep areas
12. French Park		
Short Loop	1.3	rolling; few hills
Long Loop	2.0	hilly
13. Pleasant Ridge	2.2	rolling; long hill
14. Mt. Airy Forest & Arboretum		
Arboretum Walk	2.0	rolling
Forest Loop	4.0	hilly; steep areas
15. LaBoiteaux Woods	2.0	hilly
16. Spring Grove Cemetery	3.8	rolling
17. Avon Woods Outdoor Education Center		
Big Loop Trail	.75	hilly
Creek Trail	.25	hilly
Wildflower Trail	.2	graded; rolling
18. Xavier University/Avondale	2.0	hilly; steep areas
19. Hyde Park	2.8	rolling
20. Ault Park/Observatory Historic District	3.0	rolling

Hike	Mileage	Terrain
21. Mariemont	2.4	flat
22. Terrace Park	3.2	flat
23. Kelley Nature Preserve	1.0	flat; few hills
24. Milford	2.4	rolling
25. Cincinnati Nature Center		
Powel Crosley Lake Trail	.8	rolling
Avery's Run Loop	1.8	hilly
Stanley M. Rowe All-Person's Trail	.6	flat; paved
Lookout Trail	3.0	rolling; few hills
26. The Oxbow	1.0-4.0	flat
27. Shawnee Lookout Park		
Miami Fort Trail	1.5	hilly; steep areas
Little Turtle Trail	2.0	hilly; steep areas
Blue Jacket Trail	1.3	hilly; steep areas
28. Mitchell Memorial Forest		
Wood Duck Trail	1.3	flat
29. Harrison Memorial/Congress Green	.5	hilly; steps
30. Sayler Park	3.8	flat; few hills
31. Embshoff Woods & Nature Preserve		
Parcours Fitness Trail	1.0	rolling
32. Mt. Echo Park		
Nature Trail Loop	1.0	hilly; steep areas
Park Loop	1.25	rolling
33. Clifton	5.2	rolling
34. University of Cincinnati	2.0	rolling
35. Fairview Park	1.7	hilly; steep areas
36. Over-the-Rhine/Liberty Hill	1.2	hilly; steep areas
37. Plum St./Central Parkway/8th St.	1.8	flat
38. Skywalk/Fountain Square/Fifth St.	2.0	flat; some steps
39. Cincinnati Riverfront/Lytle Park		
Historic District	2.6	flat; some steps
40. Eden Park	2.8	rolling; few hills
41. Mt. Adams	1.4	steep hills; steps
42. Alms Park/Mt. Lookout/Tusculum	4.6	hilly; steep areas
43. Lunken Airport		
Hike/Bike Trail	6.2	flat
44. Magrish Riverlands Preserve	1.2	flat; some steps
45. California Woods Nature Preserve		
California Junction Trail	1.25	hilly
Combined Loop Hike	2.0	hilly; steep areas
Meadow Loop	1.5	hilly
46. Stanbery Park	1.5	hilly; steep areas

Hike	Mileage	Terrain
47. Withrow Nature Preserve		
Trout Lily Trail	2.0	rolling; some hills
Old Farm Loop	1.75	rolling
Hepatica Hill Loop	.25	hilly; steep areas
48. Woodland Mound Park		
Combined Trail (Hedgeapple/Parcours)	1.8	hilly; steep areas
Seasongood Nature Trail	.75	hilly; some steps
49. Boone County Cliffs State N.P.		
Main Trail Loop	2.0	hilly
East Boundary Loop	1.0	hilly
50. Doe Run Lake		
North Shore Trail	2.2	rolling
Loop Trail	.5	hilly; steep areas
51. Highland Cemetery Forest Preserve		
Trail #1	1.25	hilly
Trail #2	.5	hilly
Trail #3	.75	hilly
52. Devou Park		
Nature Trail	1.25	hilly; steep areas
Overlook Hike	2.2	rolling
53. West Covington/MainStrasse	2.7	flat
54. Covington Riverside District &		
Suspension Bridge	2.5	flat; some steps
55. Newport: Civic & Mansion Hill Districts	2.5	flat
56. Newport's East Row Historic District	1.6	flat
57. Bellevue/Dayton Levee Walk	3.0	flat
58. Fort Thomas Military Reservation/		
Tower Park	1.4	flat
59. Fort Thomas Landmark Tree Trail	1.1	hilly

KEY TO MAPS

Roads:

Parking Areas:

Foot Trails:

Paved Trails:

Railroads:

Lakes/Streams:

Marshes:

Forest/Woodland:

Rock Wall/Cliff:

Bridge/Boardwalk:

Stairways:

1 MIAMI WHITEWATER FOREST

Badlands Trail
  Distance: 1.75 miles
  Terrain: hilly; steep areas

Tallgrass Prairie Trail
  Distance .7 mile
  Terrain: rolling

Oakleaf Trail
  Distance: .75 mile
  Terrain: hilly

Parcours Fitness Trail
  Distance: 1.0 mile
  Terrain: rolling

With 2359 acres of forest, meadow and lake surface, **Miami Whitewater Forest** is the largest of Hamilton County's Parks. This extensive preserve sprawls across a wooded ridge, approximately 15 miles west of Cincinnati.

A popular destination for picnics, fishing and birdwatching, **Miami Whitewater Forest** also offers several excellent hiking trails. In addition, the Visitor Center (VC) houses natural history exhibits and a Bird Museum (B) introduces visitors to the Park's avian residents.

Directions:

From Cincinnati, head west on I-74 toward Indiana. Take the Dry Fork Exit (Exit #3), turn right (north) and drive 1 mile to West Road. Turn right, cross Dry Fork Creek and proceed to parking areas as illustrated on the map. A nominal day-use fee is charged or visitors may purchase an annual pass to all Hamilton County Parks.

Routes:

Four hiking trails offer access to the varied habitats of Miami Whitewater Forest.

Badlands Trail (1.75 miles). Perhaps the best hiking trail at the park, the **Badlands Trail (BT)** begins just west of the Bird Museum (B). Enter the forest, walk a short distance, and bear left at the fork in the trail. Heading southwest, the trail winds along a ridge before turning northward. The predominant

beech-maple-oak forest is dotted with small stands of cedar, tulip and black cherry trees. Wildflowers are abundant in early spring while Christmas ferns, honeysuckle and wild grapes are easily spotted throughout the warmer months. Resident fauna include pileated woodpeckers, barred owls, white-tailed deer and flying squirrels.

Gradually ascending toward the woodland's highest ground, the route crosses several small drainages. At the northern end of the loop the trail enters an area where stream erosion has carved a network of small ridges and shallow ravines. These earthen formations offer a miniature replica of South Dakota's "Badlands," where wind and water have sculpted countless peaks and valleys from the soft, Tertiary sediments.

After snaking eastward through these "badlands," the trail turns south, descends into a deep ravine and then climbs onto the next ridge. This pattern is repeated for two more stream crossings before the path merges with the entry trail.

Oakleaf Trail (OT; .75 mile). This loop trail begins just south of the Bird Museum (B), descending through mature, deciduous forest to the edge of the Timber Lakes. Hooded warblers, ovenbirds, yellow-billed cuckoos and eastern wood pewees are often found here in late spring and summer.

The path crosses between the lakes and then forks. Turn right, hiking along the shore of the upper lake. Kingfishers noisily patrol the wetlands throughout the year

*Winter in
"The Badlands"*

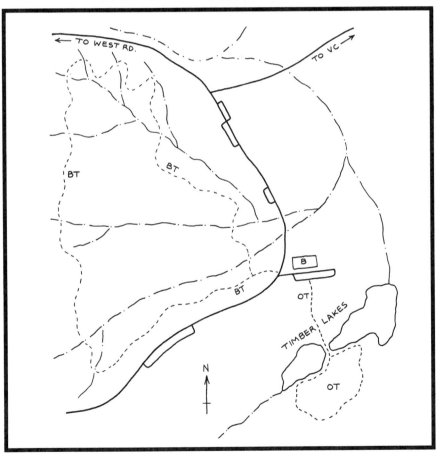

THE BADLANDS AND OAKLEAF TRAILS

while green-backed herons stalk the shallows during the warmer months. Mallards and wood ducks nest here, escorting their broods across the wooded lakes in April and May.

The trail soon curves eastward, climbing higher into the forest, and then turns to the north for a gradual descent to the shore of the lower lake. After completing the loop, cross between the lakes and ascend to the parking lot via your entry route.

Tallgrass Prairie Trail (TPT; .7 mile). This loop hike begins along the main Park road, 1.2 miles south of the West Road intersection. Though relatively short, the route crosses through an excellent diversity of habitat.

Enter the woods and continue straight ahead at the fork in the trail. After winding through dense, immature forest the path emerges at the western edge of the Park's reconstructed prairie. Before white settlers reached the Midwest, a vast tallgrass prairie stretched from western Ohio to eastern Kansas. This glorious ecosystem of wind, grass and sky has all but succumbed to the farmer's plow, yielding the productive "Corn Belt" of the American Heartland. Only small remnants of the original grassland still survive but "reconstructed prairies" are springing up across the region.

Miami Whitewater's tallgrass prairie was planted with big and little bluestem and other species that typified the native grassland. Wildflowers adorn the prairie throughout the warmer months, peaking in late summer. Eastern bluebirds, indigo buntings, blue-winged warblers, northern cardinals, eastern meadowlarks and orchard orioles are seasonal residents of the grassland. Red fox, eastern cottontails, deer mice and meadow voles inhabit the prairie throughout the year.

After crossing the grassland the trail re-enters the forest and descends to a stream crossing. It then curves westward through a mature woodland where a drum nest (n) has been placed for great horned owls. Winding to the southwest, the route passes a frog pond (p) and then snakes through moist, immature forest to complete the loop.

Parcours Fitness Trail (PFT; 1 mile). This double-loop path, lined with twenty exercise stations, starts across from the Park Campground, just south of the Lake. After entering the woods, the trail soon splits; the right fork stays atop the ridge, offering views of Miami Whitewater Lake during the colder months. Either route brings you to a second intersection where a short trail segment connects the trail's two loops (see map).

At the beginning of the second loop, the right fork descends via a stairway into the basin of the Lower Timber Lake; several side trails lead down to the water's edge while the main route parallels the lakeshore and then curves northward, climbing onto the ridge. Complete the loop atop the ridge and return to the parking area via either arm of the first loop.

A woodland boardwalk on the Tallgrass Prairie Trail

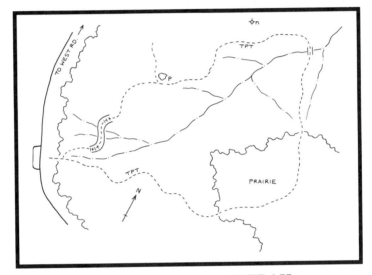

TALLGRASS PRAIRIE TRAIL

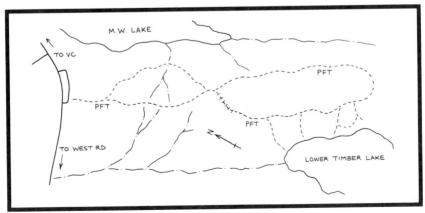

MIAMI-WHITEWATER PARCOURS TRAIL

2   FARBACH-WERNER NATURE PRESERVE

Pin Oak Trail
  Distance: .9 mile
  Terrain: flat

Most nature preserves are large tracts of abandoned or "unusable" land on the outskirts of metropolitan areas. Management often involves little more than restricting access and letting nature take its course.

More challenging is the protection and maintenance of small preserves in heavily developed areas. There, habitat destruction is continually threatened by political, economic and commercial forces. **Farbach-Werner Nature Preserve,** in the northwest suburbs of Cincinnati, is such a place.

Donated to the Hamilton County Park District by Elizabeth and Alfred Werner, the preserve was added to the Park system in 1972. Its 23 acres of field and woodland are bounded on three sides by a bustling residential and commercial zone. To the west, a small farm buffers the preserve from additional human pressure.

Farbach-Werner is a popular site for seasonal festivals and nature programs throughout the year. An **educational barn (1)** and a **nature-oriented gift shop (Nature's Niche, 2)** are on the premises.

Directions:

To reach Farbach-Werner Nature Preserve, take I-75 north and then I-275 west toward Indianapolis. Exit onto Colerain Ave. (U.S. 27) and turn left (south). Drive approximately 1.5 miles and turn right on Poole Rd. The entrance will be 1 block on your left. A daily usage fee is charged or an annual pass to all Hamilton County Parks can be obtained.

Route:

The .9 mile **Pin Oak Trail** winds through the refuge. Connecting trails permit a variable route and add to the potential length of your hike. Starting near the barn, the trail first skirts a small pond where turtles, frogs and tadpoles are easily found during the warmer months. It then loops through an open woodland before entering a small tract of forest. A **"drum nest" (3)** near the west end of these woods has been used by a pair of great horned owls; look for them in February and March.

Beyond the forest the trail follows the border of the preserve's central meadow, where wildflowers are abundant in late summer. American woodcocks use this field for their famous mating flights in early spring.

The Park District provides a trail-guide brochure that points out many of the area's natural highlights. Brochures are usually available outside the gift shop or at the trailhead. Plan to visit during each season to witness the changes of flora and fauna that characterize nature's cycle.

12

The Nature Barn houses a
meeting hall and educational exhibits.

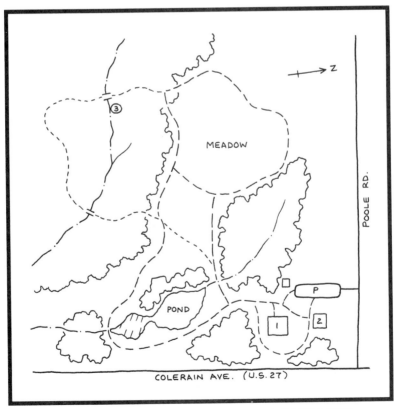

FARBACH-WERNER NATURE PRESERVE

3 GILMORE PONDS PRESERVE

Trail Network
  Distance: variable (up to 1.5 miles)
  Terrain: flat

As industrial parks and suburban sprawl threatened the open spaces of Butler County, the Izaak Walton League spearheaded the protection of **Gilmore Ponds**, a collection of ponds, marshes and seasonal wetlands southeast of Hamilton. Now managed by Metroparks of Butler County, the **Gilmore Ponds Preserve** is well known to area naturalists and provides vital wetland habitat for native and migratory wildlife.

Water levels vary widely throughout the year and the bird population fluctuates accordingly. Peak levels generally occur in March and April, attracting a good variety of migrant waterfowl. Ospreys stop by to fish on the larger ponds in late April or early May. As the flooded fields of March yield to the wet meadows and growing mudflats of spring, shorebirds stop to feed and rest on their journey to the Arctic. Rails and bitterns soon haunt the marshes and colorful warblers dart through the riparian woodlands.

Summer residents, include indigo buntings, common yellowthroats, eastern kingbirds, northern orioles and gray catbirds. Red-winged blackbirds, green-backed herons and great blue herons hunt across the marsh while kestrels and red-tailed hawks patrol the grasslands. Muskrats, opossums, raccoons, red fox and woodchucks are among the resident mammals.

Fall migrations begin by mid July as the first wave of shorebirds arrives from the Arctic. Songbird migrations peak in September and, if conditions are favorable, migrant waterfowl return in October and November.

A winter visit to **Gilmore Ponds**, devoid of pesky insects and summer humidity, can also be rewarding for the naturalist. Cardinals, song sparrows, dark-eyed juncos and yellow-rumped warblers dominate the bird population. Common snipe may flush as you stroll along the levees and white-tailed deer are often spotted on the meadows.

Directions:
From Cincinnati, head north on I-75 and then west on I-275. Take Exit #41 and drive north on Ohio Route 4 (Springfield Pike/Dixie Highway). Just over 2 miles north of I-275, bear right onto the Route 4 Bypass. Drive another 1.5 miles and turn left on Symmes Road. Proceed .5 mile and park in the small lot on your right (directly across from Beck Blvd.).

Route:
Gilmore Ponds Preserve is accessed by a network of trails that run atop earthen levees. From these elevated pathways the visitor can easily peruse the fields, ponds and marshes that characterize the preserve (see map).

The length of your walk is purely arbitrary but generally totals .5 to 1.5 miles. Be sure to bring your binoculars to fully appreciate the varied wildlife of this natural oasis. Insect repellant is strongly advised during the warmer months.

The entry trail at Gilmore Ponds

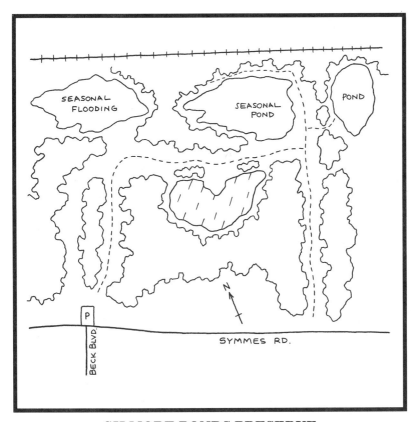

GILMORE PONDS PRESERVE

4 WINTON WOODS

Hike/Bike Trail Loop
   Distance: 2.8 miles
   Terrain: flat

Kingfisher Trail
   Distance: 1.1 mile
   Terrain: rolling; few steep areas

Parcours Trail
   Distance 1.0 miles
   Terrain: hilly

West Fork Dam
   Distance: .5-1.5 miles
   Terrain: flat

Winton Woods is both the second oldest and the second largest member of the Hamilton County Park District. Established in 1939, the Park now encompasses 2133 acres of forest, meadow and water surface. Its 188 acre lake and adjacent picnic grounds attract the majority of the annual visitors.

Directions:
From Cincinnati, head north on I-75 and then west on I-275. Take Exit #39 and drive south on Winton Road; the Park will be 3 miles ahead. Proceed to parking areas as illustrated on the map. A nominal day-use fee is charged or you may purchase an annual pass to all Hamilton County Parks.

Routes:
We suggest the following day hikes at Winton Woods.
Hike/Bike Trail Loop (HBT; 2.8 miles). Park in one of the lots off Lake Forest Circle, .7 mile west of Winton Road (see map). Follow the path as it loops westward and then eastward, straddling the north shore of West Fork Lake. Bird enthusiasts will find that these shallow backwaters attract a variety of herons and waterfowl.

Wind eastward, eventually crossing under Winton Road. The trail then loops northward, skirting an arm of the Lake, before circling the Park's central recreation area. Turn left (west) at Lake Forest Circle, cross Winton Road and continue westward to your car.

Kingfisher Trail (KFT; 1.1 miles). This loop hike starts .7 mile west of Winton Road (see map). Enter the forest, walk a short distance and bear left at the fork, descending into the Kingfisher wetland via a set of stairs. Boardwalks elevate the trail as it crosses the soggy ground and offer viewpoints into the adjacent marshland. Watch for herons, ducks and an occasional rail among the reeds. Muskrats inhabit this backwater marsh and, if you're lucky, you may spot a mink as it hunts along the bank. The wetland is named for the belted kingfishers that noisily patrol the area.

The trail leads northward along a tributary of West Fork Creek. After winding upstream for approximately 1/3 mile, the route angles to the right, climbing into the forest. It then curves southward and meanders back to the entry trail. Educational plaques, spaced along the route, illustrate some of nature's handiwork that can be found in this backwater woodland.

*The Kingfisher
Wetland*

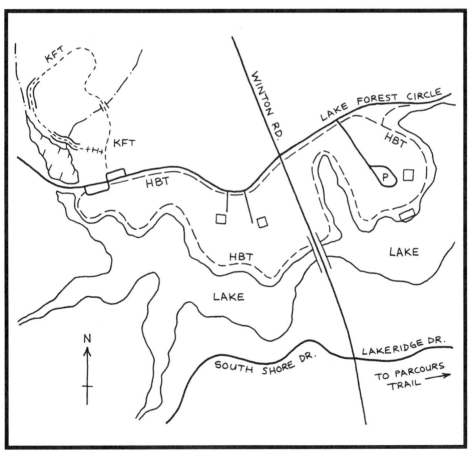

KINGFISHER & HIKE/BIKE TRAILS

Parcours Trail (PCT; 1.0 mile). This elongated, double-loop trail begins east of McKelvey Road, just south of the Lake and near the Dam (see map). From Winton Road, south of the Lake, turn east on Lakeridge Drive. Proceed .6 mile and turn left (north) on McKelvey Road. Go to the end of this road and turn right to the parking area.

The Parcours Trail leads southward, passing a baseball field and then entering the woods. After dipping across a stream the trail forks. Either route eventually brings you to a second intersection where a short connector trail leads across another stream and out to the terminal loop of the route. Bear left onto this loop, ascending a stairway and then passing between two sinkholes. The trail soon curves to the west where it reaches its high point and then angles northward, completing the loop.

Backtrack along either arm of the first loop and return to the parking lot via the original entry trail. We recommend the Parcours Trail in winter, when views extend eastward across West Fork Lake.

West Fork Dam (.5-1.5 miles). This little-known and sparsely visited section of Winton Woods offers excellent bird-watching and a pleasant stroll across West Fork Dam. From the main Park area, head north on Winton Road to Sharon Road (approximately 1 mile). Turn right (east) on Sharon Road and drive approximately 1.25 mile. Turn right on Southland Road (which becomes Sheffield), proceed .3 mile and turn right on Brunner Drive. Go one block and turn left on McKelvey Road which leads into the Park.

From the parking lot, ascend onto the levee via the private drive or via the nearby stairway (see map). Follow the path as it leads eastward and crosses the West Fork Dam. Visitors are treated to a pleasant view of the lake and of an island just south of the Dam. Swallows skim above the cool waters during the summer months and a variety of waterfowl, including wood ducks and pied-billed grebes, may be spotted on the lake. The path ends at a loop just east of the Dam.

Backtrack to the parking area. If time and energy permit, continue westward atop the levee which skirts a large meadow and ends near the lake's northern inlet. Eastern bluebirds, tree swallows, meadowlarks and northern bobwhites are often seen on the meadow, wary of kestrels and red-tailed hawks that patrol this grassland. Birders will also find an excellent variety of songbirds in the trees north of the levee.

A roundtrip stroll across the Dam and back yields a walk of approximately .75 mile. By adding in the levee north of meadow, your roundtrip hike totals 1.5 miles.

*Scene along
the Parcours Trail
at Winton Woods*

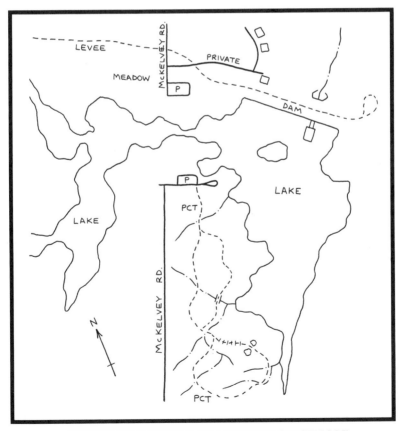

WINTON WOODS (EASTERN SECTION)

5 GLENDALE

Distance: 2.6 miles
Terrain: rolling

Glendale, Ohio, the oldest planned sub-division in our State, was initially platted by Robert C. Phillips in 1851. Six hundred acres of wooded hillside had been purchased by the Glendale Association as a residential retreat for some of Cincinnati's early industrialists. Located along the newly completed Cincinnati-Hamilton-Dayton Railroad, the village was easily accessible from the city's industrial corridor.

Incorporated in 1855, Glendale has retained its small-town, New England flavor. It's winding, gas-lit streets are lined with large, Victorian homes. Tall oak trees shade the generous lawns and small parks are spaced through the village. The **Glendale Historic District,** encompassing 392 acres, was added to the National Register of Historic Places in July, 1976.

Directions:
Follow I-75 to the Sharonville-Glendale Exit (Exit #15). Turn west on Sharon Rd. and drive 1 mile into the village. Just across the railroad tracks, turn left into the Village Square. Park here or along one of the avenues leading into the square.

Route:
Dating from Glendale's inception, the **Railroad Depot (1)** has since served as a community center, council chambers, jail and potting shop. Its use is now limited to railroad storage and maintenance. The **Iron Horse Inn (2)** occupies the former home of the Bracker Tavern, which opened in the mid 1800's.

Walk west along Fountain Ave. The small park at the intersection with Woodbine Ave. is named for William VanCleve, who willed his estate to the village for maintenance of its open spaces. Just southeast of the park is the **First Presbyterian Church (3).** The small,

buttressed structure, completed in 1860, was Glendale's first church. The larger church ws added in 1873.

Continue westward on Fountain Ave. The **John R. Wright House (4),** at Fountain & Laurel, dates from 1855. The brickwork around its arched, Florentine windows is especially attractive. The one-story frame house at **95 Fountain Ave. (5)** is the former home of Charles Sawyer, Ohio Lieutenant Governor and President Truman's Secretary of Commerce.

Cross through **Floral Park (6)** which was set aside as open space in 1851. At the top of the ridge is the **Robert's House (7),** a Classic-Revival structure dating from 1855. It reportedly served as a hiding place for slaves during the Civil War.

Continue along Fountain and turn right on Congress Ave. The Gothic, frame **Swedenborgian Church (8)** was built in 1861. Just north of the Church is the **Glendale Lyceum (9),** a social and recreational center since 1891.

The tile-roofed **Glendale Elementary School (10),** dating from the late 1800's, underwent extensive reconstruction in 1901. Across Erie Ave. from the school is the **McLean-Johnston House (11).** Built in 1855, this large, brick home was formerly a hotel and a boys school during its long career.

On the southeast corner of Congress Ave. and Sharon Rd. is **The Grand Finale (12),** known throughout the Tristate. The restaurant, which opened in 1975, is especially renowned for its desserts and Sunday brunch. Looking west along Sharon Rd. you will see the church and school of **St. Gabriel's Parish (13).** Organized in 1858, the parish's stone, Romanesque church was dedicated in 1907.

Turn right (east) on Sharon Rd. The **Town Hall and Village Firehouse (14)** date from 1875. Across Sharon Rd. from the Hall is **Glendale's War Memorial (15),** backed by a **stone, cylindrical structure (16).** The latter is a remnant of

This Italianate house dates from 1865

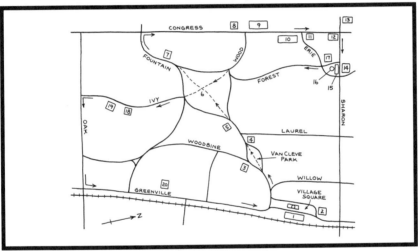

GLENDALE

Glendale's first water tower. Built in 1892, the upper tower collapsed thirty years later.

The **Episcopal Church (17)** on Forest Ave. was dedicated in 1868. One of its architects was Samuel Hannaford who also designed Cincinnati's Music Hall. Walk south on Forest Ave. which winds back to Floral Park. Cut across the park and continue south along Ivy Ave. The **Robbins House (18)**, at 780 Ivy Ave., offers a fine example of French Renaissance Revival architecture, including a mansard roof. The large, brick house at **740 Ivy (19)** is the former home of Warner M. Bateman, U.S. District Attorney for President Grant.

Turn left and descend along Oak St. A wide greenbelt, preserved along Glendale's southern border, buffers the village from nearby industrial plants.

Turn left along Greenville Ave. which parallels the railroad tracks. Many of the small, frame houses along this street were built in the 1850's, providing homes for the laborers who worked on the C.H. & D. Railroad. Contrasting with these small homes are the grand estates of the Railroad executives. The former home of Daniel McLaren, Superintendent of the Railroad, sits far from the tracks at **815 Greenville Ave. (20)**.

Returning to the Village Square, your tour of Glendale has totalled 2.6 miles.

6 WYOMING

Distance: 2.6 miles
Terrain: flat

The area that is now **Wyoming**, Ohio, was first settled around 1800. The village itself was founded by Robert Reily in 1861 and was named after a valley in northeastern Pennsylvania. Centered at the junction of three large farms (the Burns, Wilmuth and Riddle estates), Wyoming was first platted in 1869 and was eventually incorporated in 1874.

Directions:
To reach Wyoming, take I-75 to the Galbraith Rd. Exit (Exit #10-B). Drive west on Galbraith for a few blocks and turn right on Vine St., which becomes Springfield Pike. The community park will be approximately 1.7 miles on your right.

For a walking tour of this attractive neighborhood, park at the **community pool and recreation area (1)** on Springfield Pike (see map).

Route:
Walk south along Springfield Pike, the northern extension of Vine St. At the corner of Wyoming Ave. and Springfield Pike a **plaque (2)** commemorates the founding of the village by Robert Reily. Across from this intersection, at **507 Springfield Pike (3)**, is the former home of the Riddle family, built in 1835.

Walk east along Wyoming Ave. The **Wyoming Middle School (4)** occupies the south-central portion of the block. Just east of the school at **129 Wyoming Ave. (5)**, is the Stearns/Compton House, built by the founder of the Stearns & Foster Mattress Company, in Lockland. Across the street, at **132 Wyoming Ave. (6)**, is the John Wilmuth Hill House, built in 1870. The attractive house at **212 Wyoming (7)** dates from the 1890's and provides an excellent example of Queen Anne architecture. On your right, at **217 Wyoming Ave. (8)**, is a wooden, Gothic style house that served as a parsonage for over 100 years.

The **Presbyterian Church (9)**, at Burns and Wyoming Avenues, was built in 1890. This beautiful, Romanesque Revival structure was designed by Samuel Hannaford who also designed Cincinnati's Music Hall.

Turn right (south) along Burns Ave. and then right on Worthington. The first three houses on your right **(10)** are "**sister houses**," all of frame construction and initially identical in floor plan. They date from the 1860's. Farther along, the house at **200 Worthington (11)**, completed after the Civil War, affords a fine example of Italianate architectural style.

Angle to the left along Beech Ave., then left on Walnut St. and finally left on Elm Ave. At the intersection of Elm and Burns Avenues, look to the south for a view of **Wyoming Baptist Church (12)**. This white frame building, topped by an attractive gray and red, shingled steeple, was completed in 1882.

Walk north along Burns Ave. The house at **233 Burns (13)** dates from 1865. From the corner of Burns and S. Cooper, one can see the white-pillared, Italianate **Gideon-Palmer House (14)**. Perched on a hillock, this striking home was built in the 1860's and remained in the same family through four generations.

Turn right (east) on S. Cooper and then left along Grove Ave. The **300 block of Grove (15)** is characterized by colorful, frame, Victorian houses. All date from the 1890's and were built as twins or triplicates. The block seems to be an early, more appealing predecessor of our modern, repetitive subdivisions.

Proceed north along Grove Ave., turn left on Wyoming Ave. and then right on Burns. Walk 1 block and turn left on Wilmuth. This handsome block is characterized by a blend of Victorian and Tudor homes, all blessed with spacious, shaded lots.

Turn right (north) along Springfield Pike and return to the community park. Your walking tour of Wyoming has totalled 2.6 miles.

"Sister houses" along Worthington Ave.

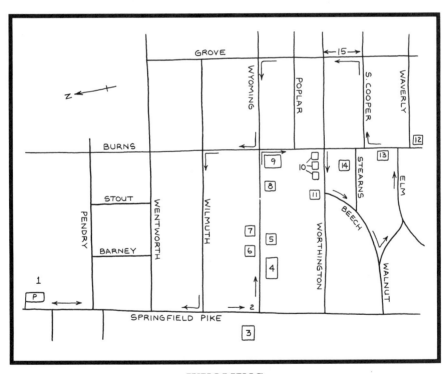

WYOMING

7 SHARON WOODS

Gorge Trail
  Distance: 1.25 miles
  Terrain: hilly; steep areas

Hike/Bike Trail
  Distance: 2.8 miles
  Terrain: rolling

Established in 1932, **Sharon Woods** is the oldest of Hamilton County's Parks. Its 737 acres of forest and meadow, centered around a 35 acre lake, provide recreation for thousands of visitors each year. In addition, the historic **Sharon Woods Village**, a collection of restored 19th Century buildings, offers a taste of Cincinnati's rural past.

Directions:
From downtown Cincinnati, head north on I-75 and then east on I-275. Take the Mason-Sharonville Exit (Exit #46) and turn right (south) on Route 42. Proceed .5 mile and turn left (east) on Kemper Road. The Park's north entrance will be on your right, approximately .6 mile ahead. A nominal day-use fee is charged or you may purchase an annual pass to all Hamilton County Parks.

Routes:
Sharon Woods offers two excellent hiking trails as illustrated on the map.

Richard H. Durrell Gorge Trail (GT; 1.25 miles). Named for Professor Richard Durrell, a former Park District Commissioner, this trail loops through a beautiful hardwood forest flanking the course of Sharon Creek. The stream has cut a deep valley through the ancient bedrock, exposing cliffs of limestone and shale. Fossil hunters will find numerous bryozoans, brachiopods and trilobites in these Ordovician sea deposits. The forest's adundant wildlife includes pileated woodpeckers, broad-winged hawks, barred owls, flying squirrels and eastern chipmunks.

Park in the small lot just east of the dam (see map). Walk back across the dam and enter the trail on the west side of Sharon Creek. The trail roller-coasters along the gorge wall before angling sharply to the right and ascending the ridge via a wide switchback. At the top an overlook yields a stunning view of Sharon Creek as it snakes through the gorge.

After a short course along the ridge, the trail descends into the gorge via a series of wooden stairways. Turn left at the trail intersection, crossing a bridge that spans Sharon Creek. Leading northward, the path skirts the Park's golf course and gradually ascends along the eastern wall of the gorge. Halfway along this section, an overlook provides a view of one of the streams many waterfalls. Upon reaching the Park road, turn right for a short walk back to your car.

Hike/Bike Trail (HBT; 2.8 miles). During the restoration of Sharon Lake, which occured in the late 1980's, the Park's paved hike/bike path was improved substantially. Alternately hugging the shoreline or cutting through adjacent woodlands, this trail circles the Lake, crossing its feeder streams via a series of fine bridges. Access to this loop is most convenient at the Park's Marina lot.

Descend from the Marina lot to the lake basin and follow the paved trail as it leads northward, passing under Kemper Road. Hugging the west shore of Sharon Lake, the route eventually loops under I-275, crossing the north inlet. It then curves eastward to cross a second inlet before passing back under Kemper Road.

Now across from the Marina, the **Hike/Bike Trail** forks. The path on your right stays near the lakeshore but ends a short distance down the valley (see map). The main route curves to the east, climbing steadily and then crossing a Park road. It

Sharon Lake

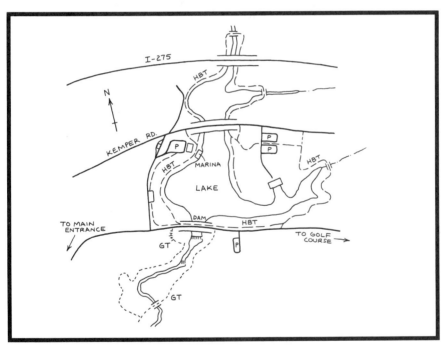

THE GORGE & HIKE/BIKE TRAILS

then continues eastward between two parking lots, enters an immature woodland and soon angles sharply to the right, descending toward the east inlet. After crossing the stream the path climbs along the edge of the golf course and emerges from the forest near the main Park road.

Paralleling this road, the trail leads to the west, crosses the Dam and then splits once again. Bear right, descending to the lake basin and follow the shoreline back to the Marina.

8   LITTLE MIAMI SCENIC TRAIL

Distance: 22 miles paved; 22 miles unpaved
Terrain: flat

The headwaters of the Little Miami River lie in west-central Ohio, just east of Springfield. The stream winds to the southwest, cutting a narrow gorge west of Clifton before crossing the farmlands of Greene County. In Warren County it flows through a deep valley which gradually widens as the River enters the southern counties of Ohio.

Designated a National Scenic River, the Little Miami is a mecca for canoeists, fishermen and naturalists. With the opening of the **Little Miami Scenic Trail,** access to hikers and cyclists has been greatly improved.

This Trail, stretching for 44 miles from Milford, Ohio, to the Spring Valley Wildlife Area (near Waynesville), offers a scenic avenue for hikers and cyclists throughout southwest Ohio. Much of the Trail follows the abandoned bed of the Little Miami Railroad which first chugged through the valley in the 1840s. The Buckeye Trail, a 1200+ mile loop through our State, incorporates the **Little Miami Scenic Trail** in its route.

Now paved from Milford to Morrow, the Trail's southern half is often congested with cyclists on warm weather weekends. Hikers may thus want to plan their visit on a weekday or during the colder months; alternatively, consider using the unpaved Trail, north of Morrow.

Directions:

The most popular access point for the **Little Miami Scenic Trail** is in **Loveland.** From Cincinnati, follow I-71 North and then I-275 East. Take the Loveland-Indian Hill Exit (Exit #52), turn left (north) and drive 3 miles into Loveland. Turn right on Loveland Avenue, cross the bridge and turn left at the second street (Railroad Avenue). Free parking is provided.

To reach the **Morrow trailhead,** take Exit #32 from I-71 and follow Ohio 123 southeast for 5.5 miles into Morrow. Turn right on U.S. 22, proceed 4 blocks and turn right on Center St. A large parking area stretches south from Morrow's old railroad depot.

The **Mather's Mill Access** is reached by taking Exit #36 from I-71 and then heading west on Warren County Road 7. Drive 1.5 miles, descending to the River; the lot is on the east bank.

The **Ft. Ancient River Access** lot is reached by taking Exit #32 from I-71. Head east for less than .5 mile and turn left (northeast) on Route 350. Descend into the Little Miami Valley, cross the River and turn right into the lot.

From **Milford, Ohio,** the Trail is accessed at the intersection of U.S. 50 and Route 126 (see map).

Routes:

There are numerous potential day hikes along the **Little Miami Scenic Trail.** The following routes are suggested.

Loveland to Foster (7 miles roundtrip). Most of this section stays near the River but views are best in winter. Foster, a small town on the Little Miami's west bank, is just beyond the picturesque U.S. 22 bridge.

Milford to Loveland (8 miles one-way). Using two cars, this is a long but relatively easy day hike. However, much of the route is away from the River and cyclists congest this section on warm weather weekends.

Morrow to Ft. Ancient (5 miles one-way). A good way to escape the parade of cyclists is to head north from Morrow, using the unpaved trail. By using two cars, a pleasant 5-mile hike can be achieved.

Ft. Ancient to Mather's Mill (2.5 miles roundtrip). This section passes through the most scenic portion of the Little Miami gorge and crosses under Ohio's highest bridge, the I-71 span.

*Scene along
the Little Miami*

**THE LITTLE
MIAMI SCENIC
TRAIL**

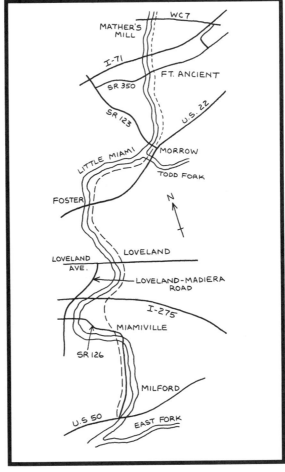

9   MONTGOMERY HISTORIC DISTRICT

Distance: 2.0 miles
Terrain: flat

Montgomery, Ohio, was first settled in 1795 when six families arrived in the area from the town of Montgomery in Orange County, New York. Among these pioneers was Nathaniel Terwilliger who officially planned the village in 1802. Incorporated in 1910, Montgomery gained "city" status in 1971.

During the past two decades, **Montgomery** has experienced phenomenal growth and residential areas have exploded across its theretofore rural calm. In an effort to preserve its historic structures and pioneer heritage, city officials have promoted a restoration of **Montgomery's Historic District** and have ensured that new buildings blend with its 19th Century flavor. Indeed, Montgomery was one of the first communities in the State of Ohio to appoint a "Landmarks Commission" to preserve and protect its historic buildings. Eight structures within the Historic District are now listed on the National Register of Historic Places.

Directions:

To reach Montgomery's Historic District, take Exit #14 from I-71 and head east on the Cross County Highway. Follow Montgomery Road north into the central village area, turn left on Cooper Road and proceed to Swaim Park (see map).

Route:

For a 2-mile walking tour of the **Montgomery Historic District**, park in the lot at Swaim Park, which is bordered by Cooper and Zig Zag Roads. The Park is a remnant of Swaim Fields, a golf course that succumbed to Montgomery's population explosion.

Follow the walkway to Zig Zag Road and turn right. The frame house on the northwest corner of Cooper and Zig Zag

dates from 1832. Known as the **Wilder/Swaim Farm House (1)**, it was built by James and Susan Wilder who moved to the area from Rhode Island. It is now home to the Montgomery Historical Society.

Turn left (east) on Cooper Road. The home at **7786 Cooper (2)** dates from 1830, having been built by Montgomery's first postmaster, Joseph Taulman. Across the street, at **7789 and 7795 Cooper Road (3 & 4)**, are two buildings that depict the "salt-box" style of architecture; they date from 1817 and 1807, respectively. Further along, the **small building (5)** at Cooper & Shelly Lane was Montgomery's first civic building, serving as village hall and jail from 1925 to 1969.

Turn left along Montgomery Road. One of Cincinnati's main arteries, this road follows the route of an early stagecoach line. Many of Montgomery's most popular shops and restaurants line its walkways, occupying structures that have graced the avenue for over 150 years. The **Pioneer Building (6)**, at 9433 Montgomery, dates from 1819 while the **Crane-Conklin Building (7)**, at 9463-65 Montgomery, was built in 1820. The **Universalist Church (8)** has occupied its prominant location since 1837 and, like the two previous buildings, is listed on the National Register of Historic Places.

Turn right along Remington, walk one block and turn right on Main St. The **Jonathan Crain House (9)**, at 9441 Main, was built in 1845. Both Main St. and Cooper Road follow the route of old Indian trails. The **"Yost Tavern" (10)**, circa 1809, sits on the northwest corner of these two streets.

Turn left on Cooper Road and walk one block to the Indian Hill line. Cross the street and backtrack along Cooper. The

28

*The Wilder/Swaim
Farm House*

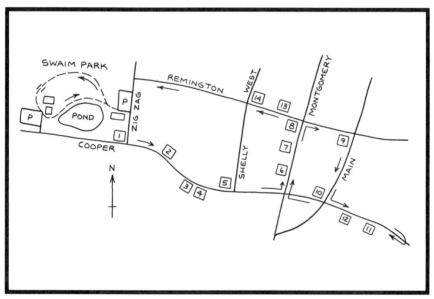

MONTGOMERY HISTORIC DISTRICT

Victorian **"Choate House" (11)** at 7967 Cooper Road, dates from 1890 while the **"Patmore/Lumley House" (12)**, at 7919 Cooper, was built in 1810.

Walk north along Montgomery Road and turn left on Remington. The **"Smethurst House" (13)** used to occupy the northwest corner of Montgomery and Remington; when its preservation was threatened by construction of the new corner building in 1991, the old frame house, which was built in 1865 for the local shoemaker, was moved one lot west and was turned to face Remington Road. The **"Blair/Barker House" (14)**, at 7844 Remington, dates from 1875. Continue west on Remington, turn left on Zig Zag, and return to Swaim Park.

10 SEYMOUR NATURE PRESERVE

Distance: 1.5 miles
Terrain: hilly

Formerly the site of a military barracks, the 80 acres of **Seymour Nature Preserve** was donated to the Cincinnati Recreation Commission by the U.S. Government in the 1970s. Cleanup of the site was spearheaded by Clair Rumpke and initial development of the trail system occured in the early 1980s.

The 1.5 mile trail loop was improved in 1992 and the Nature Preserve is open to public use. Most of the refuge, which stretches across the west wall of the Mill Creek Valley, is covered by third-growth, hardwood forest.

Directions:

From I-75, take the Paddock Road/ Seymour Avenue Exit (Exit #9). Turn west on Paddock Road and, just beyond the underpass, angle left onto North Bend Road. Drive approximately 1.5 miles and turn left on West Seymour. The parking lot will be .25 mile, on your right.

Route:

From the parking lot, the trail descends toward a stream via a winding route and two stairways. Beyond the first stream crossing the trail forks; bear left and you will soon ford the creek once again via a wooden bridge.

The trail angles westward, paralleling and then crossing the creek on stepping stones. It then climbs through a ravine, makes a sharp left turn and soon reaches a ridgetop; the path is a bit obscure within the ravine and at the left turn (watch for logs that edge the route).

Hike atop the ridge to a fork in the trail; the left trail leads out to an overlook while the right fork (the main trail) passes between log barriers and leads eastward across the ridge. The route soon descends from the ridge, crossing a stream on another wooden bridge, and then angles to the southeast, completing the loop. Turn left and return to the parking lot via the entry trail.

A November scene at the Preserve

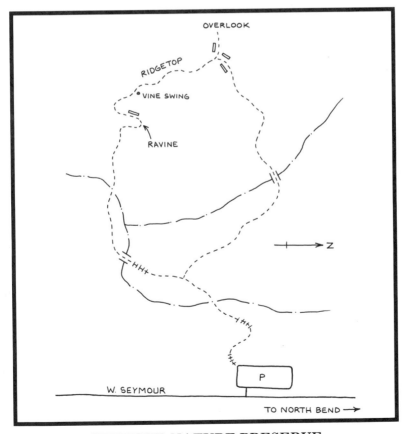

SEYMOUR NATURE PRESERVE

11 CALDWELL PARK

Distance: 1.4 miles (variable)
Terrain: hilly; steep areas

Draped over a series of ridges and ravines, **Caldwell Park's** forest preserve covers 133 acres, flanking the west bank of the Mill Creek. Access to this beech-maple woodland is via a network of trails, maintained by the Cincinnati Park Board. The primary route, dedicated in July, 1976, is named for Ray Abercrombie, the first scoutmaster of Boy Scout Troop 14.

This forest preserve was actually set aside as park land back in 1914, a donation from the descendants of Major James Caldwell. During its early years, much of the park was utilized as a nursery and orchard, supplying plant seedlings for other Cincinnati parks.

Directions:

Take I-75 to the Paddock Rd./Seymour Ave. Exit (Exit #9). Turn west on Paddock Rd. Just beyond the underpass, angle left on North Bend Rd. Drive approximately 1 mile to the forest preserve parking lot, on your right. A Nature Center, operated by the Cincinnati Park Board, sits adjacent to the lot. The center is utilized for educational programs.

Route:

Follow the **Abercrombie Trail (1)** which begins just north of the parking area. Walk about 100 yards and bear right, descending into the ravine. Cross **Ravine Creek** and turn left along this **trail (2)**. Wind uphill through a dense woodland and bear right at the intersection. Climb higher into the forest via a stairway.

Emerging onto an abandoned service road, turn right and pick up the **Abercrombie Loop Trail (3)**. Bear left at the fork and follow this trail as it winds along

the ridgetop. The mature, open forest permits broad views into the adjacent ravine.

Continue to the east end of the loop where an overlook yields a panorama of the Mill Creek Valley. The view is more expansive in winter when leaves have dropped to the forest floor. Continuing around the end of the loop, watch for a **faint trail** on your left **(4)** that leads to another overlook.

Return to the Abercrombie Loop for a short distance and then turn left, descending into the ravine. A **log stairway (5)** will be noted across the creek. It leads up to the **High Bush Loop (6)** and **Black Locust Trail (7)**. Of interest is the fact that Ravine Creek disappears beneath the surface above this junction, resurfacing further down the slope where it is fed by natural springs.

Turn right following the **Ravine Creek Trail (2)** as it winds upstream. Returning to the intersection where you previously climbed to the service road, bear left, cross the creek and ascend a short stairway. Follow this section of the **Abercrombie Trail (1)** as it loops back to the east, snakes along the ridge and returns to the parking lot. Your hike through the forest has totalled 1.4 miles.

Many of Caldwell Park's trails are partially overgrown during the summer months. To avoid this "closed in" season and to escape the insects and humidity of the mid-summer months, we recommend a visit from October through early May. The numerous maples provide a colorful display in autumn and the hilly terrain is ideal for birding in the spring. Resident mammals include gray squirrels, raccoons, chipmunks, skunk and flying squirrels. The latter are best seen at dusk.

As an addition to the route discussed above, you may wish to include the **Pawpaw Ridge Loop (8)** which leads through mature forest to another overlook. This loop will add .5 mile to your hike.

The Abercrombie Trail

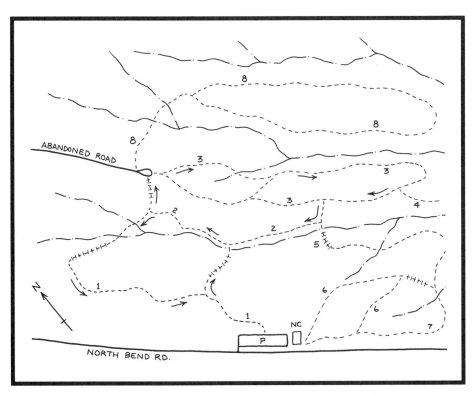

CALDWELL PARK NATURE PRESERVE

12 FRENCH PARK

Short Loop
Distance: 1.3 miles
Terrain: rolling; few steep areas

Long Loop:
Distance: 2 miles
Terrain: hilly

French Park, in Amberley Village, is a popular spot for family picnics in the summer, kite flying in the fall and sled riding in the winter. Its 276 acres spread across a gentle slope, half covered by open lawns and half by a beautiful hardwood forest.

The Park was donated to the city of Cincinnati by the late Herbert G. French, whose vast estate was known as Reachmont Farm. The **French house (5)** still sits on the property, its second floor utilized as office space by several conservation groups.

Directions:

From I-71, take the Ridge Road North Exit (Exit #8B). Drive north on Ridge Road for approximately 2 miles, passing through Pleasant Ridge. Turn right (east) on Section Road; the Park entrance will be a short distance, on your left. Park in one of the lots near the entrance (see map).

Routes:

An extensive network of trails provides access to the forested areas of French Park. The following loops are suggested.

Short Loop (1.3 miles). From the parking lot, walk along the Park road, cross the bridge and angle down along the creek through the play/picnic area. The trail starts across the creek, heading northeast. It bisects a secluded picnic area and then enters the forest, winding along the stream. Fifty yards into the woods, a spur trail crosses the creek for a short distance and then rejoins the main path upstream.

Once past this alternate loop, watch for a small **grave marker (1)** on your left. The weathered plaque pays tribute to "Sammy, Nick, Pete, Pal and Robert, faithful friends of Reachmont Farm." Continue eastward

along the north side of the creek. Bird-watching can be excellent here and fossil buffs will enjoy perusing the Ordovician rocks that jut from the steep banks. Numerous small waterfalls are spaced along the creek, their muffled gurgling adding to the peacefulness of this woodland.

Near the east end of the Park the trail splits into three routes (see map). The trail that leads straight ahead ends in a residential area. The trail to your left is used for the **Long Loop Hike** (see below). Turn right, cross the creek and climb through the forest, eventually leaving the woods across from the hilltop **picnic shelter (2)**. From this open ridge the visitor has a broad view of the Mill Creek Valley to the west, backed by the high ground of Mt. Airy and Finneytown. Sunsets can be spectacular from here.

Descend along the Park's central drive. Halfway down is a cluster of buildings... a **service barn (3)**, the **caretaker's house (4)** and the **French House (5)**. The latter serves as headquarters for Rivers Unlimited, the Hillside Trust Little Miami Inc. and the Sierra Club. Continue down the road to your car, completing a 1.3 mile loop.

Long Loop (2 miles). This route utilizes the creekside trail as described for the Short Loop. However, at the east end of the Park, bear left onto the trail that climbs northward via a stairway. Passing a residential area, on your right, the trail curves gradually to the northwest, crossing several drainages. It then intersects a wide, grassy path; turn left and follow this route as it snakes westward atop the ridge. Bypass a side trail (on your left) and continue on the

*The French
House*

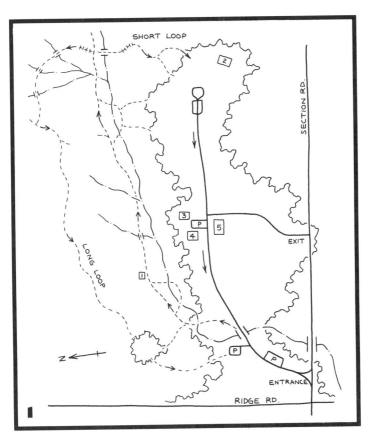

FRENCH PARK

wide path to a clearing where the trail splits. The fork to your left descends steeply to intersect the creekside trail (see map); continue straight ahead on the right fork which winds down to one of the parking areas.

13 PLEASANT RIDGE

Distance: 2.2 miles
Terrain: rolling; long hill

The territory that is now **Pleasant Ridge** was first settled in 1795. Col. John McFarland arrived from Pennsylvania and constructed a fort ("McFarland Station") to protect his fellow immigrants from the local Indian tribes. These early settlers were enamored with the area's "pleasant" views, especially those from their ridgetop cemetery. The village thus adopted the name of **Pleasant Ridge**.

During the early 1800's, the Wood family acquired much of the land in the area and, around 1825, renamed the settlement "Crossroads." This title reflected the town's location at the intersection of a major stagecoach route (now Montgomery Rd.) and a long-established Indian trail (Ridge Rd.) When the area was surveyed for construction of a narrow-gauge railroad, during the mid 1800's, the community was once again referred to as **Pleasant Ridge**. Finally incorporated in 1891, the village was annexed by Cincinnati in 1912.

While the health of its business district has fluctuated over the years, the neighborhoods of **Pleasant Ridge** have retained the quiet charm of an earlier era. Indeed, some of the older sections have witnessed a resurgence. For a walking tour through one of the village's more attractive areas, we suggest the following route.

Directions:
To reach Pleasant Ridge from other areas of Cincinnati, follow I-71 and take the Ridge Rd. Exit (Exit #8). Drive north on Ridge Rd. for approximately 1 mile, crossing Montgomery Rd. Proceed another ¼ mile and turn right onto Harvest Ave.

Park along Harvest Ave. near its junction with Ridge Rd. (see map).

Route:
Walk north along Ridge which was once part of "Columbia Rd." The latter, completed in the 1790's, stretched from Kennedy Heights to Carthage. Across Ridge Rd. are several Victorian homes, each set far from the street and beautifully restored.

Turn right onto Beredith Place which is also lined with renovated homes. This street was renamed during World War II, reportedly during a movement to abolish "German" titles from the village. The current name blends the first names of two sisters, Beryl and Edith, who lived in the neighborhood. Jog to the left as Beredith Place crosses Kincaid Rd. (see map). Continue eastward along Beredith which curves to the right and becomes Parkman Place.

Angle sharply to the left, ascending along Grand Vista Ave. Lined with stately homes and huge shade trees, this street is perhaps the epitome of upscale living. Sitting far from the avenue and well-spaced by broad, manicured lawns, many of these mansion-like homes enjoy a sweeping view of the Mill Creek Valley to the west. At the end of this street, one residence proves that a mans home can be his castle.

Circle back along Grand Vista, Parkman Place and Beredith Place. Turn Left on Kincaid Rd. for one block and then right onto Harvest Ave. Returning to your car, your stroll across the Ridge has totalled 2.2 miles.

Along Grand Vista Avenue

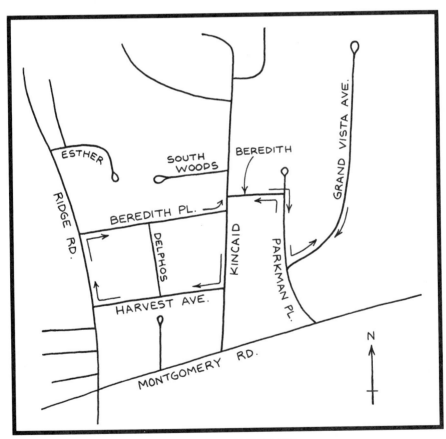

PLEASANT RIDGE

14 MT. AIRY FOREST & ARBORETUM

Forest Loop
  Distance: 4 miles
  Terrain: hilly; steep areas

Arboretum Walk
  Distance: 2 miles
  Terrain: rolling

Mt. Airy Forest, spreading across 1466 acres on Hamilton County's highest ridge, harbors over 10 miles of hiking trails. While the Park's open areas provide numerous picnic sites, its woodlands, resulting from America's largest municipal reforestation project, offer a true backcountry experience.

The Forest is also home to a fine **Arboretum** which features over 1600 species of shrubs and trees. This preserve, covering 120 acres, occupies the northern rim of the Forest and is a popular destination for botanists and birdwatchers alike.

Directions:

Mt. Airy Forest is northwest of the downtown area. Follow I-75 to I-74 west. Exit onto Colerain Avenue (Exit #18) and head north. Drive approximately 1 mile to the Park entrance.

Those interested in the Forest Loop hike should enter the Park on Trail Ridge Road; proceed .9 mile to the lot for Picnic Area #21, on your right.

Those interested in the Arboretum Walk should enter the Park on Blue Spruce Road. Bypass the Arboretum entrance road and proceed another .2 mile to a graveled lot and picnic area on your right (see map). A marker directs you to a trail that winds through the forest to the Arboretum.

Routes:

There are numerous hiking opportunities at Mt. Airy Forest. We suggest the following routes.

Forest Loop (4 miles). From the lot at Picnic Area #21, enter the woods via one of two connector trails (see map). Turn left on the **Furnas Trail (FT)**, also called the

Overlook Trail, which snakes along the ridge, high above Cedar Ravine. The trail circles Area 22 and then loops through Scotch Pine Ravine. At Area 23, Ponderosa Ridge, the path enters a clearing where a lookout shelter offers a broad view of the I-74 valley.

Re-enter the forest and bear left on the **Ponderosa Trail (PT)** which is blazed with white paint; the **Quarry Trail (QT)** splits to the right, descending into White Ash Ravine. Stay on the Ponderosa Trail which parallels the ridgetop, crossing through a beautiful area of open, mature forest. At the next trail intersection, bear right, crossing a creek.

The trail then snakes through the upper reaches of White Ash Ravine, fording small tributaries and cutting through a thicket-choked woodland. Bear left at the intersection with the **Quarry Trail (QT)** and wind higher along Stone Steps Ridge (Area #19). A parcel of open, pine forest offers a pleasant respite from the dense, humid woods.

Continue straight ahead through the next intersection and descend into Linden Ravine. Here, again, the mature forest has a pleasing openness, yielding broad views into the ravine. Passing Area #18, the trail curves right, crossing Linden Creek via a bridge. Loop around Hidden Ridge (Area #16) and descend into Red Oak Ravine.

Cross the creek and turn left, ascending along the **Red Oak Trail (ROT)**, which ends at the Park's Oval. Walk across the Oval and pick up the **Twin Bridge Trail (TBT)**. This trail is a wide path that enters the forest just to the left of the radio tower (R).

Hike along Sunset Ridge for approximately .25 mile and watch for a multi-trail

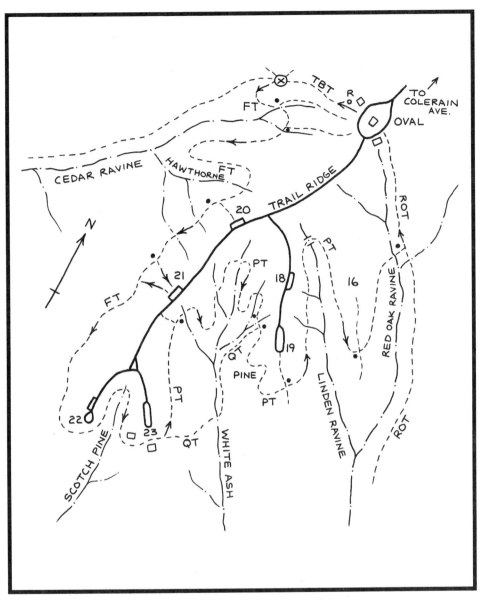

MT. AIRY FOREST LOOP HIKE

intersection, centered around a sinkhole (X). Turn left and pick up the **Furnas Trail (FT)**, marked with blue and white slashes. Loop through the upper reaches of Cedar and Hawthorne Ravines, bearing right where spur trails lead up to Trail Ridge Road. Passing Area #20, ascend along the ridge wall, cross two small streams and watch for the connector trail to Area #21; this path is immediately across from a trail sign (see map). Climb to the Area 21 lot, completing a 4 mile hike.

Arboretum Walk (2 miles). From the lot at Picnic Area #1 along Blue Spruce Road, enter the forest on a path that winds down to a stream crossing and then ascends to the edge of the Arboretum (see map). Turn left, following the wood margin and winding through a fine collection of viburnums, azaleas and rhododendrons; a **Wildflower Trail (WT)** loops through the forest just east of these shrubs.

Continue southward past dogwoods and a stand of red pine before crossing to the other side of the central lawn (see map). Turn north along the west edge of the lawn, passing white pine, Norway spruce and European larch along the way. The Arboretum's wide variety of plantlife makes it a superb destination for birdwatchers throughout the year. Berry-producing shrubs attract cardinals, catbirds, thrashers, mockingbirds and cedar waxwings in late summer and fall. The numerous conifers are a magnet for chickadees, nuthatches, siskins and finches while the rich, deciduous forest teems with warblers, vireos, flycatchers and tanagers during the warmer months.

Stop by the **Arboretum Center,** constructed in 1956, which is the focal point of horticultural and education activities at the Arboretum. The Arboretum itself was conceived in 1930 and plantings began two years later; initially sponsored by the Federated Garden Clubs of Cincinnati & Vicinity, the 120-acre Arboretum is now managed by the Cincinnati Park Board. For information regarding tours, contact the horticulturalist at 541-8176.

From the Center, follow the Arboretum Road eastward to the **Helen Meyer Lake and Rara Flora Garden.** Constructed in 1976, this garden features a one-acre, spring-fed lake, surrounded by rare trees and shrubs; the latter include Japanese maple, weeping needle juniper, Canadian hemlock and tri-color beech. After enjoying this peaceful oasis, hike westward along the forest margin, crossing through plantings of holly, lilac and boxwood and return to your car via the entry trail.

The Ponderosa Trail at Mt. Airy Forest

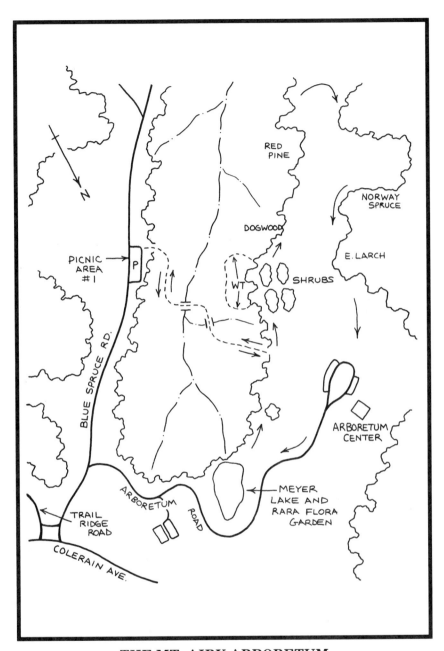

THE MT. AIRY ARBORETUM

15 LABOITEAUX WOODS

Loop Hike
   Distance: 2 miles
   Terrain: hilly

The 62 acres of **LaBoiteaux Woods,** which spread across two ravines on the west wall of the Mill Creek Valley, were donated to the city of Cincinnati by the family of Charles LaBoiteaux in 1945. Mr. LaBoiteaux, who lived on Hamilton Avenue, was an amateur naturalist who cherished the peace and beauty of this urban oasis.

From 1945 through 1960 the preserve was used as a summer camp and a wagon-drawn voting booth served as a camp office. The present Nature Center building, which houses offices and natural history exhibits, was constructed in 1960, coverting the Woods to an Outdoor Education Center. The facility is managed by the Cincinnati Recreation Commission.

A fine network of trails provide access to the hardwood forest which is buffered from Mill Creek industries by the vast territory of Spring Grove Cemetery.

Directions:
From I-75, just north of downtown Cincinnati, exit west onto I-74. Take the Elmore St./Spring Grove Exit (Exit #19) and proceed straight through the stoplight on Powers St. Turn left on Spring Grove Avenue, proceed two blocks and turn left on Hamilton Avenue (U.S. 127). Drive 2.3 miles and turn right on Hillcrest Road. Proceed one block and turn right on Lanius Lane which leads to the LaBoiteaux Woods parking lot. A small day-use fee is charged.

Route:
The following route yields a day hike of approximately two miles.

From the west side of the Nature Center building, descend a stairway to the **Old Lanius Lane Trail (OLT).** Turn left on this trail, walk a short distance and descend to the **West Creek Trail (WCT)** which leads southeastward along the stream.

Bypass the **Steps Trail (ST),** continuing down to the **Lower Creek Trail (LCT)** which angles to the west. Climb gradually upstream, bypassing the **Falls Trail (FT)** and you will ascend to the **East Creek Trail (ECT)** via a stairway. This trail heads northwestward, climbing along the east wall of a ravine. Nearing the top of the hill, the route crosses the stream and curves back to the south.

Take the first cutoff on your right, ascending a short stairway and turn right at the next intersection. This path soon curves to the left and climbs another stairway; turn right at the top of the stairs and continue northward, soon emerging from the forest at the south end of the Nature's Center's field.

As is evident from the map, there are many alternatives to the route described above. Regardless of which route you choose, plan to stop along the way to enjoy the sights and sounds of this beautiful forest. If possible, stop by the **Nature Center** building before your hike; its fine exhibits will introduce you to the flora and fauna that characterize this urban refuge.

The Nature Center Building opened in 1960

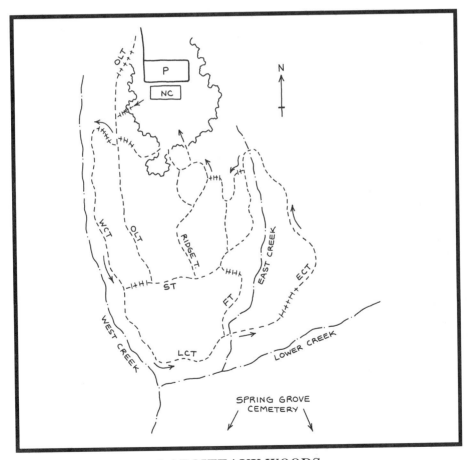

LABOITEAUX WOODS

16 SPRING GROVE CEMETERY

Distance: 3.8 miles
Terrain: rolling

Most of us do not think of a visit to the cemetery as a pleasant way to spend an afternoon. However, a stroll through **Spring Grove**, rich in history and natural beauty, is certainly an enjoyable experience. Initially conceived by Dr. Daniel Drake and designed by Howard Daniels, land was set aside for burials in 1845. The Cemetery has since gained national recognition for both its interred citizens and its spectacular landscape. Indeed, **Spring Grove** has been designated a National Historic Landmark. Sprawling over 733 acres of wooded hillside, this is the largest private nonprofit cemetery in the United States.

Directions:

Follow I-75 and take the Mitchell Ave. Exit (Exit #6). Turn west on Mitchell and then south (left) on Spring Grove Ave. The Cemetery entrance will be approximately ½ mile on your right. A complete map of the grounds is available at the gate house.

Park in the lot adjacent to the old **Administration Building (1)**. This Gothic structure dates from the mid 1800's.

Route:

Walk through the tunnel and bear right, following the green-lined roadway. One of the first recognizable names is the **gravesite of the Carew family (2)**, near **Sylvan Pond (3)**. Farther on your left, bald cypress trees line the shore of **Cedar Pond (4)**, their "knees" rising above the water's surface. On your right is the family mausoleum of **Judge Jacob Burnet (5)**, a U.S. Senator and author of Ohio's first Constitution.

Angle left from the green road to see the tomb of **Nicholas Longworth (6)** whose vineyards sprawled across Mt. Adams (then Mt. Ida) in the early 1800's. He resided in the Martin Baum House which would later become the Taft Museum.

Return to the green road, wind uphill a short distance and then angle onto the drive that loops past the **White Pine Chapel (7)**. Continue along this drive until it deadends into the white-lined road. Turn right, following the white road as it winds higher into the Cemetery.

After walking approximately ¼ mile you will pass between a **woodland (8)** and a **pond (9)**. Bear right along the white road as it runs atop a ridge, yielding a broad view to the south.

At the next intersection turn left onto the yellow-lined road. Walk a short distance and continue straight ahead on the unmarked drive (see map). Continue on this road which eventually curves up to the right, ascending to **Spring Grove's overlook (10)**. From the overlook one has a beautiful panorama of the Cemetery and Mill Creek valley and the hills beyond. University of Cincinnati buildings poke above the Clifton Ridge. The view is especially impressive in October, when fall colors blaze across the valley.

Descend from the overlook, pick up the white road and then switch to the yellow road just past the **pond (11)**. Continue along the yellow road, crossing another **pond (12)**, and passing through an open section of the Cemetery. Lower on the hillside the clustered monuments resume, including the grave of **William H. Alms (13)**.

Turn left between **Willow Water (14)** and **Maketewah Pond (15)**. Mute swans, Canada geese, mallards and migrant waterfowl are often found in this area. The grave of **Andrew Erkenbrecker (17)**, founder of the Cincinnati Zoo, is located just north of the **Cascade Pool (16)**.

Continue along the northern rim of **Geyser Lake (18)**. On your right is the grave of **Charles W. West (19)**, founder of the Cincinnati Art Museum. Across from the West monument is the tomb of **Salmon P. Chase (20)**, former U.S. Senator, Ohio Governor, Secretary of State for President Lincoln, and Supreme Court Justice.

*One of many
lakes at
Spring Grove*

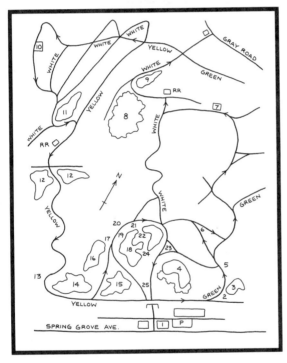

**SPRING GROVE
CEMETERY**

Farther along is the ornate, Gothic Revival mausoleums of the **Dexter family (21)**, built in 1869. Adolf Strauch, Spring Grove's superintendent and landscape architect from 1855 to 1883, is buried on the **island (22)** in Geyser Lake.

Turn right, descending along the white-lined drive. On your left is the **Soldier's Monument (23)**. Cast in Munich, Germany, in 1865, this bronze statue honors Cincinnatians who died in the Civil War. To your right, the **Fleischmann tomb (24)**, modeled after the Greek Parthenon, sits along the northern shore of Geyser Lake. Near the bottom of the slope is the grave of **General William H. Lytle (25)**, adorned with an eagle and laurel-draped column. He is one of 37 Civil War Generals buried here.

Pass through the tunnel and return to the parking lot. Your walking tour of Spring Grove Cemetery has totalled 3.8 miles.

45

17 AVON WOODS OUTDOOR EDUCATION CENTER

Big Loop Trail
   Distance: .75 mile
   Terrain: hilly

Creek Trail
   Distance: .25 mile
   Terrain: hilly

Wildflower Trail
   Distance: .2 mile
   Terrain: graded; wheelchair accessible

The 22 acres of **Avon Woods Outdoor Education Center** are covered with a luxurient hardwood forest. Established in 1970, the preserve is managed by the Cincinnati Recreation Commission and is accessed by three trail loops; these three trails are easily combined to yield a pleasant, 1.2 mile walk.

Located in the midst of a bustling residential neighborhood, **Avon Woods** is a magnet for many species of suburban wildlife. Jim Farfsing, Coordinator of Outdoor Education for the Cincinnati Recreation Commission, reports that the Woods are an excellent site for warbler watching in the spring.

Directions:

From either I-75 or I-71, take the Norwood Lateral to the Paddock Road Exit (Route 4). Head south on Paddock Road and drive .8 mile to the entrance road, on your right. Wind across the golf course to the Nature Center parking lot.

Route:

The **Creek Trail (CT)** enters the woods north of the **Nature Center** building. Bear right as you wind through a picnic area and you will soon descend to the creek via a long stairway. Turn left at the creek, crossing and then re-crossing the stream. At the next intersection a trail comes down from the picnic area (see map); cross the creek and wind up the west wall of the ravine, soon merging with the **Big Loop Trail (BLT)**.

Bear right and hike southward atop a low ridge. Continue straight ahead at the fork and also bypass the cutoff to Avon Woods Lane. The **Big Loop Trail** eventually crosses the creek and climbs onto the opposite ridge via a stairway. Curving back to the north, you will notice a side trail on your right; this old trail, not currently maintained, descends through a parallel ravine, climbs onto its eastern wall and intersects the **Wildflower Trail (WT)** (see map).

Continue along the **Big Loop Trail** which leads northward atop a ridge. Nearing the end of the ridge the trail cuts back to the southwest, crosses the main creek and ascends a stairway to intersect the entry route. Turn right, bypass the **Creek Trail** and walk out to the **Nature Center** building, crossing above the creek.

Pick up the **Wildflower Trail (WT)** on the south side of the Nature Center and complete this short loop which ends at the parking lot. Your combined hike through Avon Woods has totalled 1.2 miles.

*A stream crossing
at Avon Woods*

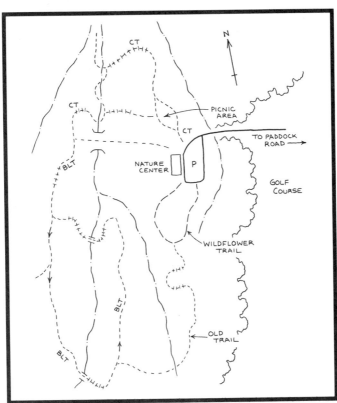

AVON WOODS NATURE PRESERVE

18 XAVIER UNIVERSITY/AVONDALE

Distance: 2.0 miles
Terrain: hilly; few steep areas

Xavier University was founded in 1831, at which time it was called the Athenaeum. Renamed St. Xavier College in 1840 (in honor of St. Francis Xavier) the school moved to its Avondale campus in 1919. Xavier achieved University status in 1930 and now offers more than 40 undergraduate majors in its three colleges. An all-male college for most of its existence, Xavier became co-educational in 1969.

Directions:
From I-71, take the Montgomery Rd./Dana Ave. Exit (Exit #5). Drive west on Dana Ave. for approximately 1 mile and turn right on Ledgewood (see map).
Park along Ledgewood Drive near Victory Parkway (see map).

Route:
The following 2 mile walk combines a tour of the University with a stroll through the adjacent neighborhood of Avondale.
Walk north along Ledgewood, ascending into the hillside community.
Avondale has perhaps had more names than any other area in the city. After purchasing the land in 1802, William McMillan called the area his "Home Plantation." James Cory named the ridge "Locust Grove" when he assumed title but "Clintonville" was the accepted name by 1852. After much of the land was acquired by the Cincinnati & Chicago Railroad, H.C. Freeman, engineer and surveyor, was sent to inspect the area. It was he who bestowed the name of "Avondale" in 1854. The village had been incorporated in 1853 and was eventually annexed to Cincinnati in 1896. Following annexation, an influx of residents from the Cincinnati basin led to rapid growth of the neighborhood.
Angle left onto Avondale Ave. and then bear left along Winding Way. Walk 1 block and turn right, climbing higher into Avondale via Lenox Place. This attractive neighborhood is characterized by huge, castle-like homes, spacious, shaded lawns and wide, gas-lit streets. It has long been home to prominent Cincinnatians, offering a green, urban retreat above the industrialized valleys.
Near the top of the ridge, turn left on Redway Ave., descending toward Victory Parkway. Walk 1 block and turn right along Dakota Ave. which ends at Dana Ave. Turn left on Dana and descend further to Victory Parkway. One of our city's more attractive boulevards, the Parkway is adorned with flower beds during the warmer months.
Turn left (north) along Victory Parkway. Corcoran Field, former home of Xavier's football team, was recently demolished and the **site (1)** is now utilized for soccer and other field sports. Continue north to the **Rev. Paul O'Connor Sports Center (2)**, which opened in 1976. This complex houses a swimming pool, basketball courts, weight room, handball and volleyball courts.
Cross Victory Parkway and ascend the stairs to Xavier's central campus area. **Hinkle Hall (3)** and **Alumni Hall (4)** are the University's oldest buildings, completed in 1920. Walk south along the front of these buildings for a sweeping view of the Avondale ridge to the west.
Angle left around Alumni Hall and walk north through the **University Mall**. The **McDonald Library (5)**, on your right, opened in 1967. Further along, a statue of d'Artagnan (Charles II DeBatz Castelmore) graces the entrance to **Albers Hall (6)**. D'Artagnan was a Captain-Lieutenant with the first company of Musketeers who died in the service of King Louis XIV of France, in 1673. The **statue (7)** was sculpted in Auch, France, and was a gift to the University by the Class of 1962. Xavier adopted the Musketeer mascot in 1925.
Continue northward through the mall, past **Alter Hall (8)**, completed in 1960 and the **Logan Chemistry Building (9)**, which opened in 1953. Bear to the right, walking

Castle-like homes are found throughout Avondale.

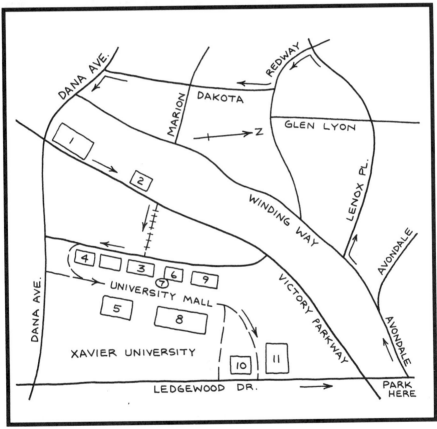

XAVIER UNIVERSITY/AVONDALE

between the **St. Robert Bellarmine Chapel (10),** dedicated in 1962, and the **University Center (11),** completed in 1965. Turn left along Ledgewood Drive and return to your car.

19 HYDE PARK

Distance: 2.8 miles
Terrain: rolling

Hyde Park, with its attractive homes, shaded streets and upscale shops, is certainly one of our more popular and fashionable neighborhoods. Incorporated in 1896, the village was annexed by Cincinnati in 1903.

Directions:

To reach Hyde Park, follow I-71 to the Montgomery Rd./Dana Ave. Exit (Exit #5). Turn east on Dana Ave. and proceed to Madison Rd. Jog to the left, crossing Madison, and continue east on Erie Ave. to the Square.

For a walking tour of Hyde Park's central corridor, park at the village square, located at the intersection of Erie Ave. and Edwards Rd.

Route:

A small park, centered around the **Kilgour Fountain (1)** divides Erie Ave. as it crosses the Square. The fountain, dedicated in November, 1900, is a gift from the John Kilgour family. Mr. Kilgour, a prominent businessman and landowner during Hyde Park's development, was president of the Cincinnati Street Railway Company. At the southeast corner of the Square is the **Engine Company No. 46 Firehouse (2),** which has served the community since 1907.

Walk east along Erie Ave. At the corner of Erie Ave. and Shady Ln. is **St. Mary's Church (3),** built in 1917. Its Classic Bedford-stone construction was modeled after the Old English Gothic churches of the 13th Century. St. Mary's parish was established in 1898 and its school was founded by Monsignor Patrick Hynes in 1908.

Further east, on the northeast corner of Erie Ave. and Paxton Ave., is the **Church of the Redeemer (4),** an Episcopal congregation founded in 1908. Having earlier used the Town Hall at Michigan and Erie, the congregation moved to its current site

upon completion of the Church in 1950.

Continue east on Erie Ave. and turn right on Grace Ave. Ahead of you, at Grace and Observatory, is the Hyde Park Community **United Methodist Church (5).** This English Gothic Church, completed in September, 1927, occupies the former site of the Mt. Lookout Methodist Episcopal Church which has been on the corner since 1880. The latter congregation merged with the Hyde Park Methodist Episcopal Church during the 1920's, forming the present day congregation.

Walk westward along Observatory Rd. This street follows the route of a 1790's stage line, which stretched from Walnut Hills to Chillicothe, Ohio. **Hyde Park School (6),** at Edwards and Observatory, opened in 1900. It currently teaches grades K through 6.

Continue west on Observatory past several blocks of stately homes. The **Cincinnati Country Club (7)** flanks the western end of the road. Established in 1895, it is the oldest golf club west of the Appalachians. The Club, which encompasses 122 acres, was incorporated in 1903.

Turn right along Madison Rd. **Wulston Triangle Park (8)** is on your right, wedged between Observatory and Erie. Across Madison Rd. is **Withrow High School (9).** Opened in September, 1919, the school was originally called East Side High. In 1924 it was renamed in honor of John M. Withrow, retired President of the Cincinnati School Board. The school's 27 acre campus, acquired by the Board in 1913, was once part of the Erkenbrecker estate. Withrow's bell tower and the nearby bridge date from the school's inception. The bridge was restored through the efforts of the Class of 1981 and was renamed in honor of Nora Mae Nolan, a former teacher at Withrow.

Turn right (East) along Erie Ave. and return to Hyde Park Square. Your walking tour of this vibrant neighborhood has totalled 2.8 miles.

Hyde Park Square

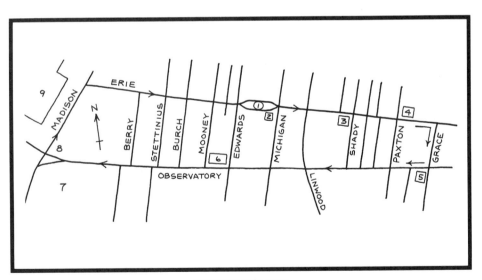

HYDE PARK

20 AULT PARK/OBSERVATORY HISTORIC DISTRICT

Distance: 3.0 miles
Terrain: rolling

Ault Park is one of Cincinnati's most popular and beautiful retreats. Its 236 acres, donated to the city by the Levi Ault family, spread across a ridge, bordering the Little Miami Valley.

Directions:

Take I-71 to the Dana Ave. Exit (Exit #5). Turn east on Dana Ave. Crossing over Madison Rd., this street becomes Observatory Rd. which ends in Ault Park.

Route:

Park near the **Pavilion (1)**. From its rooftop portico, one has a wide panorama of the Little Miami Valley to the east and of Ault Park's magnificent gardens, immediately west of the Pavilion. In the distance, University of Cincinnati buildings poke above the western horizon.

On of south side of the Pavilion is a memorial to **Levi Ault (2)**, dedicated in 1911. Descend from the this hillock and follow Observatory Circle around the north side of the gardens (see map). Bear right along Observatory Rd. which leads out of the Park. Re-entering the residential zone, proceed for a few blocks and turn right on Observatory Place.

This immediate neighborhood has been designated the **Observatory Historic District**. Victorian, Greek Revival and Transitional homes line the block, dating from 1877 to 1923. At the end of Observatory Place is the **Cincinnati Observatory (3)**. Completed in 1875, the building's dome was reconstructed in 1895. It now houses a 16 inch refractor

telescope, offices and an astronomical library. It is open to the public by special arrangement only. Cincinnati's original Observatory, dedicated in 1843, was located at the top of Mt. Adams, the current site of the Holy Cross Monastery. The Observatory was moved to Mt. Lookout when the glow from our burgeoning city began to interfere with use of the telescope.

The smaller observatory, southeast of the main structure, is the **Mitchell Building (4)**. Designed by Samuel Hannaford and Sons, it opened in 1908. It harbors an 11 inch telescope and is used for educational programs.

Walk along Avery Ct. (see map) to Wellston Place. Turn left along Wellston, cross Observatory Rd. and continue on Park Ridge Place. At Griest Ave., turn left for ½ block and then left again on Suncrest Dr. This street winds upward and eastward, intersecting Herschel Ave. Turn right along Herschel, passing **John Kilgour Elementary School (5)**. Continue southward for a few blocks and turn left on Principio. This street leads back into Ault Park, entering along its southern ridge.

Near the Park entrance you are rewarded with a fine view of Lunken Airport to the south. Before returning to your car, stroll through Ault Park's beautiful gardens which offer one of Cincinnati's most spectacular floral displays from April through September.

Your walking tour through the park and its nearby scenic neighborhoods has totalled 3.0 miles.

The Ault Park Pavilion

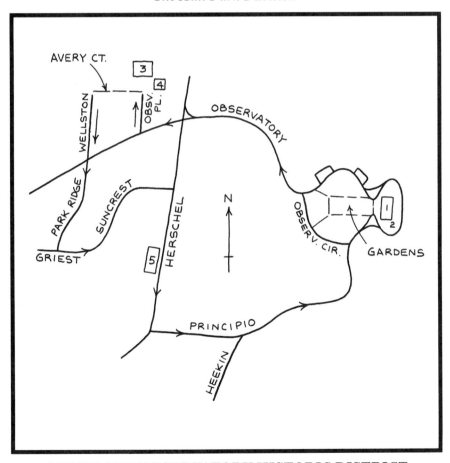

AULT PARK/OBSERVATORY HISTORIC DISTRICT

21 MARIEMONT

Distance: 2.4 miles
Terrain: flat

Most towns and villages form gradually over many years as homesteads cluster near a convenient or attractive site. In contrast, **Mariemont**, east of Cincinnati, was conceived and almost totally planned by Mrs. Mary Emery and her family. Designed to resemble an Old English village, Mariemont's construction began in 1922. The village was eventually incorporated in 1941.

Directions:
From Cincinnati, follow Columbia Parkway (U.S. 50) east. Columbia Parkway becomes Wooster Pike. Mariemont Square will be approximately 9.5 miles from the Downtown area.

For a 2.4 mile walking tour of this clean and inviting community, park in the central square at the intersection of Wooster Pike and Miami Rd.

Route:
At the west end of the square is the **Mariemont Inn (1)** which has served the village since 1926. A popular site for receptions and other social gatherings, the Inn's sixty overnight units are all unique in design and all furnished with antique furniture.

Follow Madisonville Rd. which angles to the northwest. Walk several blocks and turn left along Plainville Rd. The large, Italianate building on your left **(2)**, complete with clock tower, is the **Parish Center** for the Mariemont Community Church. Completed in 1928, the building was originally the village recreation center. It was acquired by the Church in 1956 and now houses the parish offices, class-rooms and a pre-school.

Turn right (west) on Chestnut St. The **Dale Park Building (3)**, now a community

education center, was first used as an elementary school when it opened in 1926. **The Mariemont Community Church (4)**, dedicated in March of 1927, sits back from the southeast corner of Oak and Chestnut. Its tile roof, retrieved from a crumbling English monastery, dates from the early 14th Century.

Continue west along Chestnut St. and turn left on Beech. These blocks are lined with Tudor townhomes which characterize the older sections of Mariemont. Turn left along Wooster Pike, heading back toward the square. The 50 acre **Dogwood Park (5)** sprawls along the opposite side of the Pike. Among the trees, a stone **Bell Tower (6)** rises 100 ft. Constructed in 1929, the tower was dedicated to Mrs. Emery.

The small **War Memorial Cemetery (7)** sits on a knoll, just south of the Community Church. Several of the graves date from the 1840's. **Dale Park (8)**, south and east of the Cemetery, spreads to Plainville Rd. **Mariemont Elementary School (9)** occupies most of the next block. Completed in 1939, this building was the original home of Mariemont High School, which gave way to a Middle School in 1970. The Elementary School took over in 1983.

Continue east along Wooster Pike to the square. A **plaque (10)**, at the west end of the square, commemorates the addition of Mariemont to the National Register of Historic Places in July, 1979.

Cross to the southeast corner of the square and follow Crystal Springs Rd. (see map). Angle left onto Mt. Vernon Ave. and turn right along Miami Bluff Drive.

Across from the intersection of Miami Bluff and Center St. is a **small park and stone concourse (11)**. The latter was dedicated to Isabella Hopkins and her sister, Mary Emery, in October, 1964.

Tudor townhomes line Chestnut St.

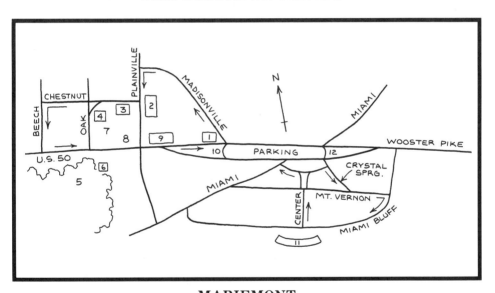

MARIEMONT

From the concourse the visitor has a broad view of the Little Miami Valley which stretches past the southern edge of the village.

Continue the walk along Center St., bear left onto West Center and then turn right along Miami Rd., which leads back to the square. At the east end of the square is a memorial to **Thomas Emery (12)**, dedicated by his wife, Mary, in December, 1955.

22 TERRACE PARK

Distance: 3.2 miles
Terrain: flat

The **Terrace Park** area was first settled in January, 1789, when Captain Abraham Covalt and a contingent of 45 adventurers arrived from Pittsburgh, Pennsylvania. Covalt constructed a fort ("Covalt Station") on the current site of **St. Thomas Episcopal Church (7)**. Created to protect the settlers from local Indians, the fortress offered limited security... Covalt himself was killed by Indians and the area's population remained sparse through the early 1800's. Completion of the Little Miami Railroad, in 1840, spurred settlement of the region and, in 1857, the Great Robinson Circus adopted the village as its winter home.

The name "Terrace Park" was apparently assigned by Jacob Tigner, a local manufacturer, in the 1870's. The village was eventually incorporated in 1893.

Over the past century **Terrace Park** has evolved into an appealing neighborhood with wide, shaded avenues. While many of its trees were destroyed by a tornado in 1969, the village launched a five-year tree restoration project, leading to it designation as "Tree City, U.S.A." in 1986 and 1987.

Tucked in an elbow of the Little Miami River, Terrace Park's flat terrain, quiet streets and attractive homes guarantee a pleasant stroll.

Directions:

To reach Terrace Park from downtown Cincinnati, follow Columbia Parkway (U.S. 50) east. This road becomes Wooster Pike as it heads up the Little Miami Valley. Entering Terrace Park, turn right at Elm Ave. This intersection, controlled by a stoplight, is approximately 14.2 miles east of the downtown area.

Park along Elm Ave. in front of the **Elementary School (1)**.

Route:

Across the street from the school is a **house (2)** that dates from 1869. Just north of this residence is **Lindell Grove (3)**, home to Boy Scout Troop 286.

Walk north along Elm Ave., cross the bridge and angle left onto Park Ave. (see map). Continue 1 block and turn right along Western Ave. to Wooster Pike. This major road, part of U.S. 50, follows the route of an old Indian trail. The Pike opened as a toll road during the mid 1800's and remained such for over fifty years. Terrace Park's first school opened in 1830 and was located in the building where the **Yankee Dollar Gift Shop (4)** now resides.

Turn right along Elm Ave. **Terrace Park's Community Center (5)** occupies a former Baptist Church, built in 1892. Purchased by the village in 1922, the Center is used for council meetings and community functions.

Cross the bridge and angle left onto Terrace Place. The **Village Green Memorial Park (6)** will be noted on your right. Walk 1 block and turn right along Rugby Ave. In sequence turn left on Yale, right on Oxford and left on Miami Ave. Directly ahead of you is **St. Thomas Episcopal Church (7)**. Built in 1907 by John Robinson as a memorial to his wife and daughter, the Church occupies the former site of a mission that was established here in 1870 by Charles Kellogg. A small plaque also commemorates the former presence of Covalt Station on this plot.

Circle to the left, following Terrace Place and Cambridge Ave. (see map). Turn right and walk south along Miami Ave. as it parallels the course of the Little Miami River. Continue for six blocks and turn right on Stanton Ave. Follow this street back to Elm Ave. and to your car. Your walking tour of Terrace Park has totalled 3.2 miles.

Terrace Park Community Center

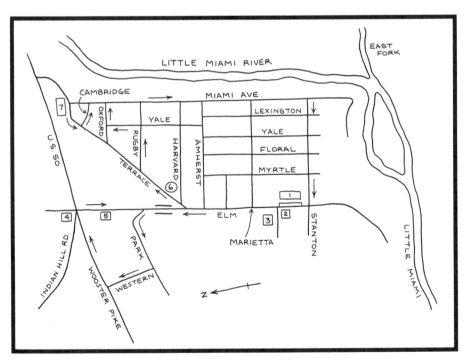

TERRACE PARK

23 KELLEY NATURE PRESERVE

Distance: 1 mile loop
Terrain: flat; few low hills

Kelley Nature Preserve, a memorial to Walter A. Kelley, is managed by the Clermont County Park District. This small but interesting preserve is characterized by floodplain woodlands, wet meadows and one of the finest reconstructed prairies in the Tristate region. Stretching along the north bank of the Little Miami River, **Kelley Nature Preserve** is a popular destination for fishermen and naturalists alike.

Directions:

Kelley Nature Preserve is 4 miles north of Milford on Route 126, just west of Miamiville.

Alternatively, from I-275 northeast of Cincinnati, take the Loveland/Indian Hill Exit (Exit #52) and head south on Loveland-Madiera Road. Drive 1.75 miles and turn left (east) on Remington Road (Route 126). The Preserve will be 1.8 miles ahead, on your right.

Route:

A network of trails provide access to the varied habitats of Kelley Nature Preserve. We suggest the following route which yields a hike of approximately 1 mile.

From the southwest corner of the parking lot, pick up the trail which cuts across a small clearing, enters the forest and soon arrives at the north bank of the Little Miami River. Turn left (east) and wind along this scenic waterway; two side trails lead down to the River's edge and benches offer peaceful reststops along the main route. Bypass cutoffs that lead into the interior of the Preserve (see map).

Nearing the eastern end of the refuge, the trail curves northward and soon emerges from the woods at the edge of the **reconstructed prairie.** Planted with grasses and wildflowers that typified the once vast tallgrass prairie of the American Midwest, the grassland is bisected with trails, permitting close examination of its flora and fauna.

Walk along the southern edge of the prairie and then cut through its center on a north-south path (see map). Jog to the east and pick up the trail that re-enters the woodland, climbing onto the wall of the floodplain. During the colder months, broad views extend from this low ridge out to the Little Miami River. A steady ascent brings you to the Preserve's entry road; turn southward through the clearing and pick up the trail as it re-enters the forest and descends onto the floodplain (see map).

Bypass the spur trail that leads toward the shelter house and continue eastward to the western edge of the prairie. Hike southward along the grassland and then return to the parking area on a trail that exits the southwest corner of the tallgrass preserve.

*The Little Miami
from Kelley
Nature Preserve*

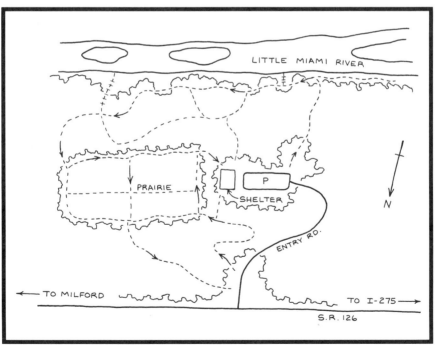

KELLEY NATURE PRESERVE

24 MILFORD

Distance: 2.4 miles
Terrain: rolling

Situated along the eastern edge of the Cincinnati metropolitan area and separated from nearby communities by the Little Miami River, **Milford,** incorporated in 1836, has retained a small town atmosphere. First settled in 1796, the village's economy was based on lumber and grist mills well into the 1900s. Even today the River plays a major role in Milford's commerce, attracting tourists and canoeists to the area.

Directions:

To reach Milford from Cincinnati, follow U.S. 50 (Columbia Parkway) east. Drive 15 miles into Milford's central business district and leave your car at **Riverside Park,** also called **Carriage Way Park (1).**

Route:

Riverside Park (1) overlooks the Little Miami River and contains a small **cemetery plot (2)** with graves dating from the mid 1800s. A dam, which diverted water to the town's mills, used to span the River near the south end of the Park.

Walk south along High St. The **Medaris House (3),** at 512 High St., was built in 1811 and underwent renovations in the 1970s. Turn right onto Main St. and descend into the business district. Many of the shops that line these streets occupy structures that date from the early-mid 19th Century. **Milford Memorial Park (4),** at Main and Sycamore, commemorates the city's war veterans; a central brick memorial was funded by the American Legion and Auxillary Post 450.

Continue southward on Main St. The **Ernst Building (5),** on the northwest corner of Main and Garfield, was completed in 1849 and served as Milford's

first Masonic Temple. Turn right along Garfield Avenue which was originally called "Cross St." when the city was platted in 1806; the street was renamed to honor President Garfield.

Turn left on Water St. which was paralleled by a sluice during the town's milling era. The last of the grist mills, which burned down on New Year's Day, 1920, stood near the River, just downstream from the U.S. 50 bridge. Milford's present-day **Masonic Temple (6)** graces the east side of Water Street and the **Old Milford Library Building (7),** circa 1835, sits on the northwest corner of Mill and Water Sts. The attractive frame building across from the Old Library was the **John Kugler House (8)** from 1827 to 1868. Built in 1816, the house was upgraded by Kugler who equipped it with Milford's first central heating system. John Kugler, one of the City's early entrepreneurs, operated a mill, a distillery, a livery stable and a general store on his riverside estate.

Milford's present-day **U.S. 50 bridge (9)** is the city's fourth bridge to span the Little Miami River; the original structure, completed in 1818, was a wooden toll bridge. Head east along Mill St. The stone buildings clustered near the intersection of Mill and Main Sts. were all built by John Kugler. The **"Corn House" (10),** now called the "Old Mill Building," was used to store and process corn prior to its use in the production of whiskey.

Continue eastward on Mill St. which ascends into one of Milford's most attractive residential areas. Restored Victorian homes, some dating from the mid 1800s, line the shaded avenues. Walk south along Mound Avenue. At Mound and Hickory is the entrance to the **S.E.M. Villa & Laurels Retirement Community (11).** The Villa

Shops along
Main St.

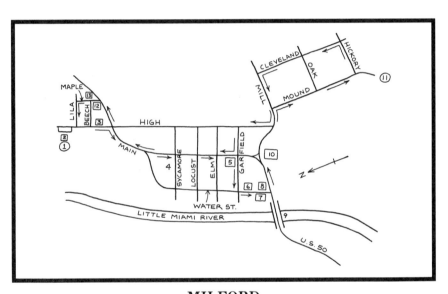

MILFORD

itself, constructed in 1929, was originally a Jesuit seminary. The seminary closed in 1969 and the property was acquired by the Southeastern Ecumenical Ministry, an organization of seventeen regional Churches. With the aid of a grant from H.U.D., the Ministry remodeled the Villa in 1971, creating 155 residential units. Since then, other buildings have been added to the retirement community.

Walk east on Hickory and then north along Cleveland Avenue. Turn left on Mill St., right on High St. and left on Garfield Avenue. Follow Main Street northward through the business district and turn left on Maple St.; the **Craver-Hookom Funeral Home (12)** dates from 1870. Across Maple St. is the **Milford Methodist Church (13),** which has occupied the site since 1936.

Turn left along Lila Avenue, returning to Riverside Park. Your walking tour of Milford has totalled 2.4 miles.

25 CINCINNATI NATURE CENTER

Powel Crosley Lake Trail
Distance: .8 mile
Terrain: rolling

Stanley M. Rowe All-Person's Trail
Distance: .6 mile (paved)
Terrain: flat

Avery's Run Loop
Distance: 1.8 miles
Terrain: hilly

Lookout Trail
Distance: 3.0 miles
Terrain: rolling; few hills

If you enjoy a walk through the woods but cannot tolerate the untamed wildness, overgrown trails and "no facility" status of many nature preserves, we recommend a visit to the **Cincinnati Nature Center.** Established in 1967, the Center now encompasses 750 acres of forest, meadow and open woodland. Well-marked manicured trails lead from the parking area to all sections of the Preserve. The Rowe Interpretive Center houses refuge offices, an exhibit hall and a nature-oriented bookstore.

Numerous potential trail routes wind through the refuge and a complete map is provided by the Center. Numbered markers, placed at trail intersections, make the maps easy to follow.

The **Cincinnati Nature Center** is open to the public on weekdays but is reserved for members on weekends and holidays. A nominal day-use parking fee is charged. For information regarding membership and activities at the Center, contact them via the address or phone number listed in Appendix II.

Directions:
Follow I-275 to the east side of Cincinnati. Take the Batavia Exit (Exit #63-B) and head east on Ohio Route 32. Drive 1.2 miles and turn left on Gleneste-Withamsville Road. Proceed .4 mile, turn right on Old S.R. 74 and go .25 mile to Tealtown Road. Turn left on Tealtown Road; the Center will be approximately 3 miles ahead, on your left.

Routes:
We suggest the following day hikes; taken together, they provide an excellent overview of the Center's varied habitats. All trail loops originate at the **Rowe Interpretive Center (RC).**

Powel Crosley Lake Trail (PCT; .8 mile). This loop hike, which corresponds to the Center's **Edge Trail,** is perhaps the most popular route at the Nature Center. It begins behind the **Rowe Interpretive Center (RC)** where a boardwalk straddles the southwestern shore of Powel Crosley Lake. The trail then winds in and out of the adjacent forest as it circles the lake. Spur trails lead out to the marshy shores where nature lovers can enjoy the myriad of creatures that inhabit this wetland.

Canada geese, mallards and red-winged blackbirds nest along the lake, wary of minks that patrol the marsh. Pied-billed grebes are often seen here during migrations and pileated woodpeckers haunt the forest throughout the year. Frogs, snails and whirligig beetles entertain children from May through September.

Refer to the map which illustrates the trail's specific route. Numbered intersection markers correspond to those used at the Center.

Avery's Run Loop (1.8 miles; hilly). This combined route corresponds to the Center's **Wildflower and Geology Trails.** Follow the Powel Crosley Lake Trail eastward from the Rowe Interpretive Center (see preceeding hike). At intersection #5, turn right on the **Geology Trail**

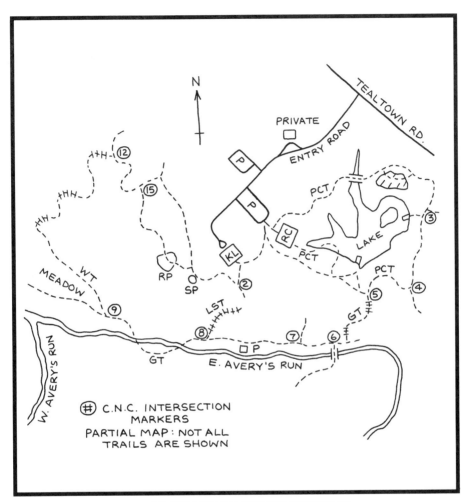

CINCINNATI NATURE CENTER

(GT), descending via stairways to the north bank of Avery's Run. Head downstream, passing intersections 6 & 7. Ordovician shales and limestones jut from the creek bed, loaded with fossils of ancient sea life. Halfway along the Geology Trail an **old pump house (P)** sits by the stream. Bypass the **Limestone Steps Trail (LST)** at intersection #8, soon crossing and then re-crossing Avery's Run.

At intersection #9, bear right onto the Wildflower Trail (WT) which hugs the edge of a meadow and then climbs through the forest via switchbacks and stairways. Turn right at intersection #12 and right again at intersection #15. Stop by the **Reservoir Pond (RP)** to enjoy its amphibious residents, curve past the **old swimming pool (SP)** and turn left at intersection #2, passing the **Krippendorf Lodge (KL)**. Continue along this trail to the parking lot.

Lookout Trail (LT; 3 miles). For a bit of solitude and diversity, try the **Lookout Trail**, most of which lies northeast of Tealtown Road (see map). From the **Interpretive Center (RC)**, head north on the west arm of the **Powel Crosley Lake Trail (PCT)** and, after crossing the north inlet, cut out to the Center's entry road. Follow this lane out to Tealtown Road, crossing the road to access the **Lookout Trail**.

The route first skirts a large hayfield, bypassing intersection #27, and arrives at the edge of **Willow Pond (WP)**. It then crosses the field and winds along the adjacent forest. Angling to the north, the **Lookout Trail** snakes atop a ridge, offering broad views of the East Fork Valley. A section of I-275 (near its junction with U.S. 50) can be seen in the distance and, during the warmer months, turkey vultures soar along the valley wall.

The return route descends through mature forest, re-crosses Tealtown Road and climbs back to the parking area, passing another pond and a private residence along the way.

Stanley M. Rowe All-Person's Trail (.6 mile; paved; SRT). Designed for persons with physical limitations, this paved route begins at the front of the Interpretive Center (RC) and heads northwest, paralleling the edge of the parking lot. After crossing the entry road the trail angles to the left.

Bypass the return route, on your left, soon passing a **bird blind (B)**. The trail now cuts through an immature woodland, emerging at the edge of a prairie/cropfield (intersection #17). Follow the southern edge of this field and turn right at the paved intersection for a short walk out to a pond; this wetland, nearly covered with water lilies, teems with green frogs during the warmer months.

Cross the boardwalk and head south on the paved trail. Turn left at intersection #18 and backtrack to the Center's entry road. Just past the **bird blind (B)**, bear right onto the paved trail as it parallels the west side of the parking lot and returns to the Interpretive Center.

Powel Crosley Lake

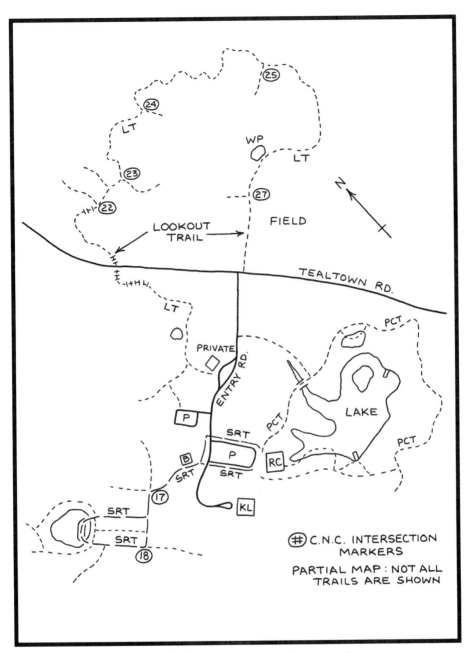

CINCINNATI NATURE CENTER

26 THE OXBOW

Distance: variable (1-4 miles)
Terrain: flat

The broad floodplain of the lower Great Miami River, which straddles the Ohio-Indiana border, has long been recognized for its fertile crop lands and its underlying wealth of sand and gravel. Only over the past decade has the valley's importance as a refuge for native and migratory wildlife been brought to the public's attention.

Seasonal flooding of the Ohio and Great Miami Rivers, usually peaking from February through early April, combined with man's construction of levees and gravel pits, has created a flat landscape of ponds, marshlands, oxbow lakes and broad, productive fields. Riparian woodlands line the permanent waterways, offering prime habitat for barred owls, red-headed woodpeckers, prothonotary warblers and belted kingfishers. White-tailed deer, raccoons, opossums and red fox are among the mammals that find refuge in these moist woods.

The flooding of late winter and early spring produces a vast network of shallow ponds and flooded fields, attracting a wide variety of shorebirds and waterfowl to the valley. Ospreys and bald eagles stop here during their spring and fall migrations and the summer months bring a superb variety of herons, egrets and marshland songbirds to these vital wetlands. Large flocks of Canada geese and ring-billed gulls winter on the floodplain, joined by mallards, black ducks, green-winged teal and great blue herons.

Aware of the valley's crucial role as a staging area for migratory shorebirds and waterfowl and learning of plans to develop an industrial port near the mouth of the Great Miami, a group of concerned citizens founded **Oxbow, Inc.**, in 1985. By soliciting public and private funds and by drawing other conservation organizations into the effort, **Oxbow, Inc.**, has purchased or obtained easments on key tracts of land across the floodplain, thereby discouraging development and protecting the vital wetlands of "**the Oxbow.**"

Named for the oxbow lake in the southeastern corner of Indiana, an abandoned channel of the Great Miami River, the entire floodplain has come to be known as "**the Oxbow.**" Persons interested in lending support to this exciting conservation project should contact Oxbow, Inc., at the address listed in Appendix II.

Visitors to the **Oxbow** will not find a network of manicured trails to lead them out to the marshes and ponds. Seasonal flooding precludes such luxury and sturdy, waterproof hiking boots are strongly recommended. Nevertheless, old farm roads and earthen dikes offer reasonable access to the wetlands, as illustrated on the map.

Directions:

The most popular area for birdwatching and "tramping around the Oxbow" is along or near the oxbow lake in extreme southeastern Indiana. To access this area, follow I-275 to its westernmost section (along the Ohio-Indiana border). Take the Lawrenceburg-Greendale, U.S. 50 Exit (Exit #16). Turn left on U.S. 50 and proceed to parking areas shown on the map.

Routes:

As noted above, there are no specific hiking trails at the Oxbow; however, old farm roads lace the area and day hikes of 1-4 miles can easily be achieved.

Most visitors to the Oxbow enter the wetlands one block south of the I-275 exit ramp, winding past a cement plant (see map). Unfortunately, much of this area

The Oxbow Lake

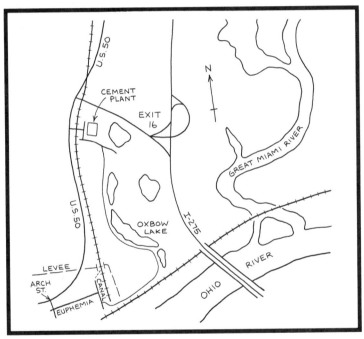

THE OXBOW

has been used as a dump and the roadside trash makes for an unpleasant introduction to the Oxbow. Should you enter here, leave your car north of the lake and hike along the dirt road that parallels its western shore, a one-way distance of approximately 1.25 miles (2.5 miles roundtrip).

For a more scenic stroll to the Oxbow Lake, continue south on U.S. 50 to Lawrenceburg and proceed to Canal St.,

as shown on the map. Leave your car near Canal & Euphemia Sts. and pick up a trail that climbs to the railroad tracks (see map). Head south along the levee to a dirt/gravel road that descends onto the floodplain, just east of a lumber mill. This road leads out to the southern end of the Oxbow Lake. The roundtrip hike from Canal St. to the Lake is approximately 3.4 miles.

27 SHAWNEE LOOKOUT PARK

Miami Fort Trail
   Distance: 1.5 miles
   Terrain: hilly; few steep areas

Little Turtle Trail
   Distance: 2.0 miles
   Terrain: hilly, few steep areas

Blue Jacket Trail
   Distance: 1.3 miles
   Terrain: hilly; few steep areas

The Shawnee ridge, rising east of the lower Great Miami Valley, is rich in human history. Long before the first white men reached the Ohio River, Indian tribes had settled along this ridge. Providing broad views of the surrounding countryside, this forested retreat offered an ideal base camp. Hunting parties found abundant game in the forest and nearby marshlands. Fish were plentiful in the Ohio and Great Miami Rivers and these streams provided access to outlying areas.

The ridge was probably first used by Paleo-hunters over 15,000 years ago. These nomadic people crossed from Asia during the Pleistocene Epoch and traversed our continent in pursuit of mammoths, buffalo and other game. They were followed by Archaic civilizations, based on a forest subsistence and more inclined to remain in one area. Among these later groups were the "mound builders" who settled along the Mississippi and Ohio Valleys. In southern Ohio, they were represented by the Hopewell and Adena cultures. Hopewell Indians lived on the Shawnee ridge from about 300 B.C. until 450 A.D. Much later, probably in the late 1600's, modern tribes, including the Miami and Shawnee, arrived in the Tristate region.

Remnants of these Indian cultures persist along the ridge today. **Shawnee Lookout Park** was established in 1967 to preserve these artifacts and to provide recreation for Cincinnatians. The Miami Purchase Association, now the Cincinnati Preservation Association, organized the effort to protect the natural and cultural riches of this historic area.

Directions:

To reach Shawnee Lookout Park from Cincinnati, follow U.S. 50 (River Rd.) west for approximately 15 miles. Entering Cleves, Ohio, turn left at the stoplight (Mt. Nebo Rd.), proceed 1½ blocks and turn right on Miami St. Follow this road as it curves to the left and parallels the Great Miami River. Drive 4 miles to the Park entrance, on your left.

Routes:

Shawnee Lookout Park provides three excellent hiking trails. Trail guide brochures are available for each and can be obtained at the ranger station.

Miami Fort Trail (A; 1.5 miles). This 1.5 mile loop originates at the end of the Park's central roadway. After ascending through the forest, the trail enters a large clearing, bordered by earthen walls. Since reclaimed by vegetation, these are the remnants of an ancient Indian fortress, constructed by the Hopewell Tribe. Burial mounds, borrow pits and other relics from their culture can be found in the surrounding forest.

Continue straight ahead at the trail intersection and proceed along the western edge of the Shawnee ridge. Several overlooks are spaced along this section of the trail, providing fine views of the Great Miami Valley. The lakes, marshlands and floodplain forest that border the Valley's croplands are home to a wide variety of birds, mammals and other creatures. Numerous migrants visit these wetlands in the spring and fall. Efforts are thus underway to preserve the Valley (known

Entering the Fort

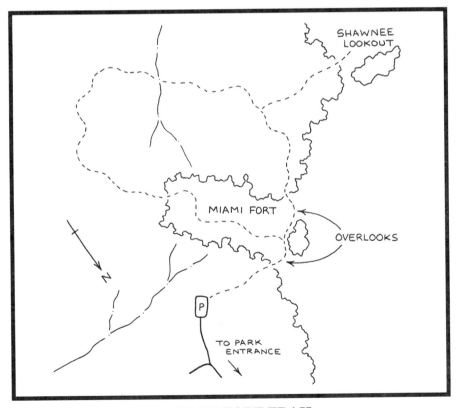

SHAWNEE
LOOKOUT

MIAMI FORT

OVERLOOKS

N

P

TO PARK
ENTRANCE

THE MIAMI FORT TRAIL

as "the Oxbow") as a wildlife refuge, free from further industrial development. Spearheaded by Oxbow Inc., local conservationists are working to protect the area by purchasing key tracts of land. For more information on this vital project see the Oxbow Inc. listing in the Appendix.

At the south end of the loop a spur trail leads out to "the Shawnee Lookout". Here, over 300 feet above the River, the visitor is treated to a spectacular view of the Ohio Valley, the mouth of the Great Miami River and the Northern Kentucky hills. The I-275 bridge spans the Ohio just west of the State line.

Return to the main trail loop and turn right. The trail dips through a steep ravine and then curves back toward the north, winding through the forest. A visit at dawn or dusk is usually rewarded by the presence of white-tailed deer that emerge from the woods to browse in open areas. Once back at the Fort, pick up the entry trail and descend to the parking area.

Little Turtle Trail (B; 2.0 miles). This 2-mile trail starts behind a playground, just across the road from a parking lot (see map). Named for a Chief of the Miami Indian tribe, the well-marked trail enters the forest, angles to the left and soon skirts a large meadow, dotted with bluebird boxes.

After hiking approximately ½ mile you will come to an intersection where the old entry trail comes in from the left (see map). Continue straight ahead, winding into a ravine and up the other side. This section is a bit steep in places but the footing is good.

At the top of the ridge you are treated to a broad view of the Ohio River Valley, unmarred by power plants or storage tanks. Other than an occasional barge or pleasure boat, the scene is pleasingly devoid of 20th century distractions.

When you must move on, hike westward along the ridge. The trail eventually curves to the north and returns to the trail intersection. Turn left and retrace your entry route to the parking area.

Blue Jacket Trail (C; 1.3 miles). Named for a Chief of the Shawnee Indians, this 1.3 mile trail starts west of the Park's central roadway, just behind a parking lot (see map). After a gentle descent through the forest, the path crosses a power-line clearing where deer often browse at dusk.

Re-entering the forest you will soon come to a fork in the trail. Bear left, hiking along the ridge and then crossing another power-line cut. Knifing into the woods, the trail winds into a ravine, crosses a small creek and ascends the opposite hillside. At the south end of the loop a clearing provides an expansive view of the forested hills that flank the Ohio Valley.

Angling to the north, the trail climbs higher and the forest opens again, yielding a spectacular view of the Great Miami Valley. As discussed in the Miami Fort narrative, the "Oxbow" wetlands before you are a vital refuge for migrant and resident wildlife.

Follow the ridge as it curves toward the northeast. Re-cross the power-line cuts and return to your car via the entry trail.

Ohio River from the Little Turtle Trail

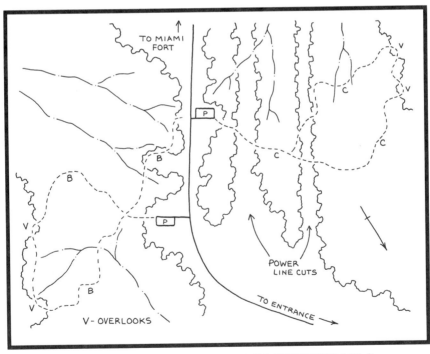

LITTLE TURTLE & BLUE JACKET TRAILS

28 MITCHELL MEMORIAL FOREST

Wood Duck Trail
Distance: 1.3 miles
Terrain: flat

Donated to the Hamilton County Park District by William Morris Mitchell as a memorial to his parents, this 1106 acre preserve is a popular destination for picnics. **Mitchell Memorial Forest** spreads across a ridgetop, just south and east of the Great Miami Valley.

Directions:
From Cincinnati, follow U.S. 50 (River Road) west to Cleves, Ohio. Turn right on Route 264. Drive approximately 3 miles, climbing onto the ridge, and turn left on Zion Road. Proceed .8 mile and bear left at the junction with Zion Hill Road (staying on Zion Road); the Park entrance will be another .8 miles, on your left. Drive past the lake and park in the lot adjacent to the Wood Duck Trailhead (see map).

Route:
The **Wood Duck Trail** meanders through a mixed woodland, skirting a meadow and crossing other small clearings along the way. The trail's destination is a secluded pond, surrounded by forest and partially ringed with a marsh.

Mallards, wood ducks and herons feed at the pond during much of the year. Mammals, including white-tailed deer, raccoons, opossum and an occasional red fox may be spotted here at dawn or dusk. Salamanders and crayfish inhabit the creek, below the dam, while frogs haunt the marshy shores.

The area is especially beautiful in spring when redbud trees dapple the woodland and numerous wildflowers adorn the trail. Honeysuckle, multiflora rose and wild grape have invaded the forest, providing food and shelter for wildlife but threatening the welfare of native plant species. Pockets of red cedar, among the first trees to reclaim distrubed areas, will be noted along the clearings.

Return to the parking lot via the same route, completing a hike of 1.3 miles.

Wood Duck Trail

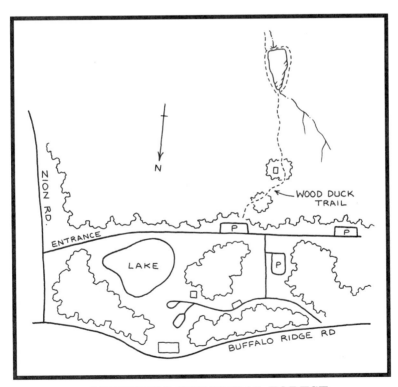

MITCHELL MEMORIAL FOREST

HARRISON MEMORIAL/CONGRESS GREEN

Distance: .5 mile
Terrain: gentle hill; some steps

William Henry Harrison, the 9th President of the United States, was first introduced to southwest Ohio in 1791 when his military duties brought him to Fort Washington. Enamored with the region, he settled in North Bend in 1814. From there he directed his political and military careers. Elected to the House of Representatives in 1816, Harrison became a U.S. Senator in 1825 and was appointed Minister to Colombia in 1828. He was nominated by the Whig Party and elected President of the United States at the age of 68, the oldest first term President until Reagan's victory in 1980. Inaugurated in March, 1841, Harrison succumbed to pneumonia 1 month later, the first U.S. President to die while in office.

President Harrison's father-in-law was John Cleves Symmes, a wealthy New Jersey jurist and Congressman who claimed most of what is now Hamilton County. Judge Symmes founded the town of North Bend, convinced that it would serve as the nidus for settlement of the Ohio Valley. Later floods would prove him wrong and the higher, drier Losantiville site gave rise to the urban center. Despite this misjudgment, Symmes' extensive land holdings ensured that he would have a profound influence on the area's development, as road, township and community titles still attest today.

A short walk across a hillside in North Bend takes the visitor back to our city's infancy and pays tribute to these historic men.

Directions:

Follow U.S. 50 (River Rd.) west from Cincinnati. Drive approximately 15 miles and turn right on Miami Ave. (watch for the sign directing you to the **Harrison Memorial**). Drive 1 block and turn left on Brower Rd. Proceed approximately ½ mile and turn right on Cliff Rd. Park in the small lot at the Memorial (see map).

Route:

Ascend the stairs and circle the **monument (1)** that rises above the tombs of William Henry Harrison and several of his family members. The elevated terrace overlooks the great North Bend of the Ohio River and the Kentucky hills beyond.

After circling the Memorial site, walk north along Cliff Rd. Approximately 50 yards up the slope a memorial to **Abraham Brower (2)** and a remnant of a **1796 mill stone (3)** will be noted to the right of the roadway. Across from these monuments a stone stairway ascends into **Congress Green (4)**, a small cemetery containing the grave of John Cleves Symmes (1742-1814) and other early settlers. Symmes' daughter, Anna, wife of William Henry Harrison, is also buried here. The central tomb, marked with a limestone obelisk, is the burial place of Betsy Basset Short, President Harrison's daughter, who died in 1846.

Returning to the parking area, your walk through history has totalled .5 mile.

The Harrison Memorial

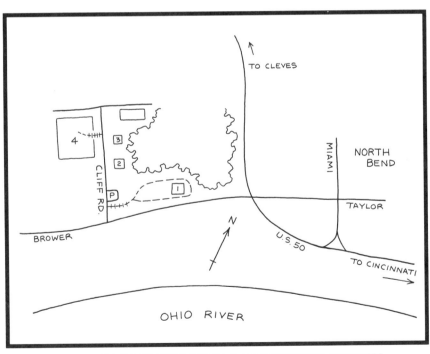

HARRISON MEMORIAL/CONGRESS GREEN

30 SAYLER PARK

Distance: 3.8 miles
Terrain: mostly flat; few hills

Sayler Park, on the banks of the Ohio River, has long been home to riverboat captains, tugboat crews and other river lovers. First settled in the early 1800s, the town of "Home City" arose by 1849. Incorporated in 1879, the village was eventually annexed by Cincinnati in 1911. With annexation the community's name was changed to Sayler Park, honoring Nelson Sayler, the town's first mayor. Annexation encompassed the adjacent towns of Fernbank and Delhi.

Directions:

To reach Sayler Park from downtown Cincinnati, follow U.S. 50 (River Road) west. Drive approximately 10 miles and bear right onto Gracely Avenue. Proceed 7 blocks to the Village Park.

Route:

For a walking tour of this riverside community leave your car at the **Village Park**. The large home at **6624 Parkland (1)**, just northeast of the park, was built in 1880. The former home of **Dr. Benjamin Lehman**, it was originally planned as a hospital.

Walk southeast along Gracely Avenue. The **First Presbyterian Church (2)** at Gracely and Twain dates from 1867. To its southeast, the **Twitchell House (3)**, built in 1860, sits behind a picket fence. Its former owner, Ernest Twitchell, invented the process of sapponification (used to make vegetable oil). Continue along Gracely, passing stately hilltop homes that command sweeping views of the River.

Turn left on Zinn Place, cross Revere Avenue and continue northeastward on Rockaway. Turn left along Home City Avenue and proceed to Twain Avenue which was platted as a boulevard. The **John McQuitty House (4)**, at 206 Twain, is one of the town's oldest homes; the McQuitty family donated the land for the Village Park.

Head northwestward along Home City Avenue. The **Sayler Park Elementary School (5)**, which instructs grades K through 6, opened in 1929. Continue along Home City for approximately 1/3 mile, turn left on Dahlia Avenue and then right on Fernbank. **Short Woods** golf course, on your right, encompasses 32 acres. An **Indian burial mound (6)** can be seen near the southern end of the property.

Continue northwestward along Fernbank, another boulevard. The town of **Fernbank**, founded by Charles Short, was incorporated in 1888. As discussed above, the village was annexed by Cincinnati in 1911, at which time it became part of Sayler Park. Turn left, descend along Overcliff and turn right on Gracely Avenue. On the hill to your right is the **Church of the Resurrection (7)**, an Episcopal Church built by Charles Short as a memorial to his parents. Completed in 1877, the Church's exterior was designed by Samuel Hannaford, the architect for Cincinnati's Music Hall.

Continue down to **Thornton Park (8)**, a tiny, mid-intersection plot centered on the **Fitzhugh Thornton Memorial**. The latter, dedicated in 1912, is the statue of an Indian, erected by Eliza Thornton to honor her deceased husband. With a total area of .01 acre, this is the smallest park in Cincinnati.

Return to your car by walking southeastward along Gracely Avenue. The **Rudolph Siegel House (9)**, at 7128 Gracely, dates from 1903. Dr. Siegel was a pioneer in the field of endodontics. Take a well-deserved break at the **Village Park**... your walking tour of Sayler Park has covered 3.8 miles.

The Village Park

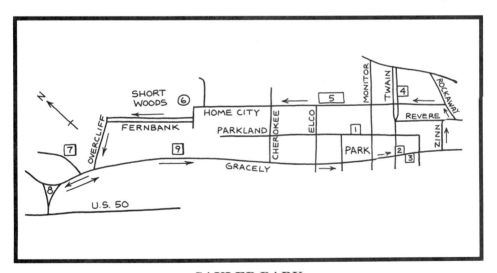

SAYLER PARK

31 EMBSHOFF WOODS & NATURE PRESERVE

Parcours Fitness Trail
   Distance: 1.0 mile
   Terrain: rolling

The term "fitness trail" usually brings to mind an oval, asphalt track, lined with chin-up bars. Embshoff Woods' Parcours route shatters that image, offering a pleasant hike through scenic terrain.

Embshoff Woods & Nature Preserve joined the Hamilton County Park District in 1982. It's 226 acres of forest and meadow stretch across a ridgetop in Delhi Township, approximately five miles west of downtown Cincinnati. Conceived by George and Margaret Embshoff, who donated the initial tract of land, much of the Preserve's territory remains in its natural state.

Directions:
   Take U.S. 50 (River Road) west from Cincinnati. Drive 2.5 miles and turn right on Fairbanks Ave. Proceed ½ mile and bear left onto Delhi Pike. Drive approximately 1.2 miles and turn left on Mt. Alverno Rd. Go one block and turn left onto St. Paul Rd. which leads into the Preserve. Park in the lot adjacent to the Parcours Trail, just across from the **River Mount Pavilion (1).**

Route:
   Parcours Fitness Trail. The first section of this 1 mile hike winds through an open woodland, skirting the Park's **frisbee golf course (2).** Cincinnati's downtown buildings loom above the eastern horizon, providing a scenic backdrop.

Crossing a service road, the trail descends into a ravine. At the bottom, turn left for a gentle ascent of the next ridge. Along the western end of the loop the trail crosses a small meadow and then re-enters the forest. Hike eastward, descending a long series of earthen steps. At the bottom the trail loops back toward the west, following the stream bed, and re-joins the entry trail. Turn left and wind back to the parking area.

For those inclined to accept the challenge, eighteen exercise stations are spaced along the Parcours Trail. Bird enthusiasts will enjoy watching the hawks and kestrels that often soar above the meadow. Other wildlife at Embshoff Woods include great horned owls, barred owls, raccoons, opossum, gray squirrels and numerous songbirds. Their continued presence reflects the success of the Embshoffs' dream.

78

April on the Parcours Trail

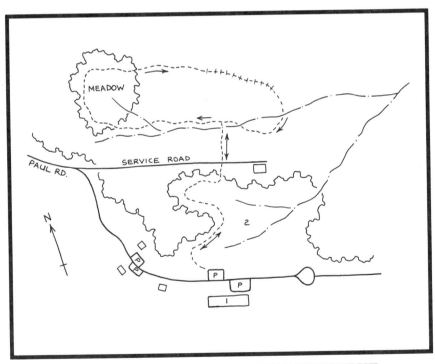

EMBSHOFF WOODS & NATURE PRESERVE

32 MT. ECHO PARK

Nature Trail Loop
   Distance: 1 mile
   Terrain: hilly; steps

Park Loop
   Distance: 1.25 miles
   Terrain: rolling

Of all the promontories that overlook Cincinnati's downtown area, **Mt. Echo Park,** at the southern end of Price Hill, yields the grandest panorama. Established in 1908, the Park spreads for 73 acres across this high ridge. From its terrace, 300 feet above the Ohio River, the visitor is treated to an expansive view of the Cincinnati basin as it fans out from the lower Mill Creek Valley. Beyond the city's skyscrapers, the highlands of Clifton, Mt. Auburn and Mt. Adams appear to fuse as a continuous ridge. Across the Ohio, the Kentucky hills rise above the riverside communities. Barges and speedboats ply the River as trains, cars and trucks roll across the many bridges.

Directions:

From downtown Cincinnati, follow 6th St. (U.S. 50) west. Keep right and exit onto Elberon Ave. which winds up the hillside. The Park entrance will be on your left, near the crest of the ridge. Follow Mt. Echo Park Road until it ends in a parking lot near a play area (see map).

Routes:

There are two potential day hikes at Mt. Echo Park.

Nature Trail Loop (1 mile). This trail begins just north of the parking lot, at the edge of the play area (see map). The path enters the woods and descends to a creek; cross the bridge and bear left, paralleling the stream. Angling away from the creek, the trail dips through a second drainage and then climbs to the ridgetop via a long stairway.

After exiting the woods, turn left and walk along the forest edge. You will soon intersect the west arm of the Nature Trail which descends through the rich, deciduous forest to a bridge. Cross the creek and bear left, climbing along a steep stairway which leads up to the parking area.

Park Loop (1.25 miles). This route uses the east arm of the nature trail, as described above. Rather than returning on the west arm, continue out to the shelter house (1) and then angle to the east, crossing the Park's baseball field (2).

Cross Crestline Avenue and hike through an open woodland that stretches across a low ridge. You will soon arrive at a stone shelter with four chimneys (3). Constructed by the W.P.A., this structure is a popular spot for family picnics. From its stone wall the visitor has a fine view of downtown Cincinnati, framed by nearby trees.

Descend the stairs to Mt. Echo Park Drive and follow the road to the Park's famous overlook (4). During the warmer months, spectacular floral gardens adorn the Park's Pavilion (5). Renovated during the 1980's, this pillared landmark is utilized for a variety of social events.

Follow Mt. Echo Park Road back to the parking lot, completing a walk of 1.25 miles.

View from Mt. Echo's Overlook

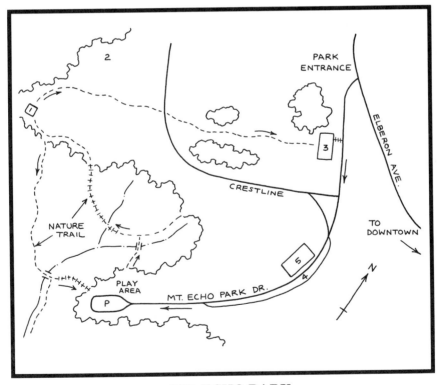

MT. ECHO PARK

33 CLIFTON

Distance: 5.2 miles
Terrain: rolling

With its stately homes and gaslit streets, **Clifton** is one of Cincinnati's most prestigious neighborhoods. First owned by Charles Clarkson, a Cincinnati merchant, most of the land north of Ludlow Ave. was then known as Clifton farm. During the mid 1800's, the land was subdivided into large estates as the first "Clifton Barons" settled in the area. Among this group were George McAlpin, James Hughes and Henry Probasco. The village was incorporated in 1850 and was eventually annexed by Cincinnati in 1896.

Directions:

To reach the Clifton area, follow I-75 and take the Hopple St. Exit (Exit #3). Turn left and follow Martin Luther King Drive as it winds up the ridge. Turn left (north) on Clifton Ave. and proceed to Mt. Storm Park, as per the map. Leave your car in the Mt. Storm parking lot.

Route:

Our 5.2 mile walking tour through Clifton begins at **Mt. Storm Park,** which was purchased by Cincinnati in 1911. Accessed via Lafayette Ave., this urban refuge is a popular spot for picnics. Mt. Storm's location, at the western end of the Clifton ridge, yields a broad view of the Mill Creek Valley.

The **"Temple of Love" (1),** on the Park's central knoll, dates from the mid 1800's. It was designed to cover a water pump though the latter was never used. Further along Lafayette, the castle-like **Bethesda Home for the Aged (2)** is perched along the ridge. Formerly known as the Scarlet Oaks Mansion, this 1867 structure was the home of George K. Schoenberger.

Turn right along Middleton Ave. which dips through the west side of "Old Clifton." **Rawson Woods (3),** a 10-acre Bird Pre-

serve, occupies the northwest corner of Middleton and McAlpin Avenues. Cross McAlpin, proceed 2½ blocks and turn right on Evanswood. Walk 1 block and turn left along Whitfield, which jogs to the right, crossing Ludlow Ave. Ludlow is the business corridor of the Clifton area, lined with shops and restaurants.

Continue south on Whitfield and then turn left on Terrace Ave. Cross Clifton Ave. and wind into the northern end of Burnet Woods (see map). **Good Samaritan Hospital (4)** looms to the west of the Park. Founded in 1852 by the Sisters of Charity, the Hospital moved to Clifton in 1915. Just south of Good Samaritan is the **Hebrew Union College (5),** established in 1875 by Dr. Isaac M. Wise. It is the oldest Jewish theologic school in the western hemisphere.

Burnet Woods was set aside as a park in 1872. It has long been a haven for University of Cincinnati students and its artificial lake attracts fishermen throughout the year. The **Trailside Museum (6)** depicts flora and fauna that can be found in Cincinnati's Parks.

Exiting Burnet Woods, cross Jefferson Ave. and continue north along Brookline until it ends. Turn left on Glenmary and proceed to Clifton Ave. **Immanuel Presbyterian Church (7),** at Bryant and Clifton, dates from 1883.

Turn right (north) along Clifton Ave. The **Church of the Annunciation (8),** dedicated in 1929, offers an excellent example of Ionic style architecture. Further north, the **Clifton Public School (9)** fills the northwest corner of McAlpin and Clifton Avenues. Completed in 1905, the school is graced by the **Probasco Fountain (10).** The latter was dedicated in 1887, a gift to the village from Henry Probasco, who also donated Cincinnati's famous Tyler Davidson Fountain.

Calvary Episcopal Church (11), at 3766 Clifton Ave., was built in 1867. This Gothic structure's spire was yet another gift from Henry Probasco, a memorial to his brother-

The Temple of Love, Mt. Storm Park

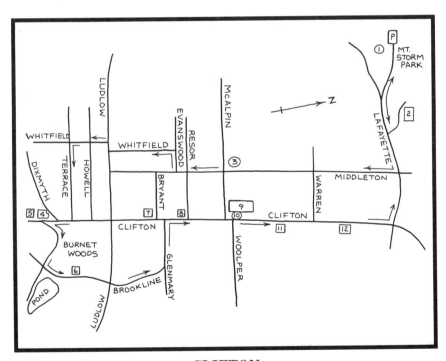

CLIFTON

in-law, Tyler Davidson. The yellow, frame house at **3874 Clifton Ave. (12)** is the former home of Robert Buchanan, President Buchanan's cousin, who moved to Cincinnati in 1823 and started a grocery business.

Turn left along Lafayette Ave. and proceed back to Mt. Storm Park, completing a scenic, historic and strenuous hike through Clifton.

34 UNIVERSITY OF CINCINNATI

Distance: 2.0 miles
Terrain: rolling

The **University of Cincinnati** is certainly the academic hub of our city. Founded in 1819, the University moved to its Clifton campus in 1895. It now sprawls across 389 acres, including the Medical Center and branch campuses.

Directions:
For a walking tour of U.C., take I-75 to the Hopple St. Exit (Exit #3). Follow Martin Luther King Drive east, winding up the Clifton ridge. Park along this road or on Brookline Drive in Burnet Woods (see map).

Route:
Walk south along Clifton Ave. The **College of Design, Art & Architecture (1)** sits on a hill to your left. Further along Clifton Ave. is **Wilson Auditorium (2)**, completed in 1932. This hall is used for concerts and plays and has long been home to the Mummers' Guild, a U.C. drama company. The west side of Clifton Ave. is lined with sorority and fraternity houses.

Bear left and ascend along the semi-circular drive (see map). Near the top, turn left and climb the stairs to the front of **McMicken Hall (4)**. This University building, the original on its Clifton campus, is named for Charles McMicken, who, upon his death in 1858, willed his estate to Cincinnati for the creation of a municipal college.

Walk southward, crossing in front of the **Old Van Wormer Library, (5)**, now the Administration Building. This structure dates from 1900. Continuing toward the south you will notice the towers of **Hughes High School (6)** in the distance. Dedicated in December, 1910, the building is one of Cincinnati's finest examples of Tudor architecture. The school is named for Thomas Hughes who left his estate to the

city for the education of its poor children.

Just past the **Teachers College (7)**, turn left and then right, passing in front of the **Carl Blegen Library (8)**. This was U.C.'s main library prior to the opening of the **Langsam Library (21)** in August, 1978. Continue between the library and the **Law School (9)** and turn left along Corbett Drive as it descends from Calhoun St. Lined with nightclubs and cafes, Calhoun St. means recreation and relaxation for U.C.'s students.

The **Patricia Corbett Pavilion (10)** sits in a bowl to your left. This complex, dedicated in April, 1972, houses a 400 seat theater, renowned for its opera productions. Its $5 million construction was funded through the generosity of Mr. & Mrs. J. Ralph Corbett. At the bottom of the slope is **Memorial Hall (11)**. This attractive, red-brick and stone building was completed in 1924. Ahead of you is **Schmidlapp Hall (12)**, built in 1911, which now serves as the headquarters for the University's R.O.T.C. program.

Turn left, ascending onto the plaza that flanks **Mary E. Emery Memorial Hall (13)**. The Hall and adjoining **Corbett Auditorium (14)** opened in November, 1967, celebrating the 100th anniversary of Cincinnati's College Conservatory of Music. This complex was also a gift from Mr. & Mrs. J. Ralph Corbett. Follow the plaza westward and then cross the elevated walkway as it angles to the right. The bridge and grassy slope that front **Tangeman University Center (15)** form the hub of student social activity during the warm days of spring and fall. The Tangeman Center, U.C.'s "Student Union," was completed in 1937.

Walk north on the path that zig zags along the west side of the Tangeman Center

*Tangeman
University Center*

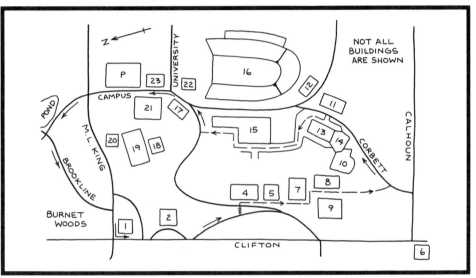

UNIVERSITY OF CINCINNATI

and then right, descending along the roadway (see map). On your left is the Renton K. Brodie Science and Engineering Complex. The building just across from **Nippert Stadium (16)** is **James A. Rhodes Hall (17)**, named for Ohio's former governor who broke ground for the vast complex in 1964. Other buildings in the complex include **Zimmer Auditorium (18)**, the **Brodie Basic Science Center (19)** and the **Crosley Tower (20)**. The entire project took over six years to complete.

Nippert Stadium (16), a home to the U.C. Bearcats, was completed in 1924. Continue down Campus Drive to University Ave. On your right is the new **University Bookstore (22)** and the **Faculty Center (23)**. Ahead and to your left is the **Walter C. Langsam Library (21)**. Dedicated in August, 1978, the building is name for Dr. Langsam, President of the University from 1955 to 1971.

Walk north along Campus Drive, cross Martin Luther King Blvd. and enter Burnet Woods. Purchased by the city in 1872, the Park's 116 acres provide a welcome retreat for University students throughout the year. Turn left at the central intersection and follow Brookline Drive back to your car. Your walking tour of the U.C. campus has totalled 2.0 miles.

35 FAIRVIEW PARK

Distance: 1.7 miles
Terrain: hilly; steep sections

Except to local residents, Cincinnati's **Fairview Park** is relatively unknown. This is unfortunate since its 28 acres offer some of the most expansive views in the city.

Deeded to the Cincinnati Park Board in 1940, the Park stretches along the southwest terminus of Clifton Heights, 300 feet above the Mill Creek Valley. Though the latter is cluttered with railyards and industrial plants, it is, in fact, the heart of Cincinnati's economy. Beyond the valley, Price Hill and Mt. Airy fuse as a continuous ridge while, to the southwest, the Ohio River glistens in the sun. South of the Park, the downtown buildings rise from the Cincinnati Basin which is bordered to the east by Mt. Adams. Northern Kentucky's hills loom along the southern horizon.

Directions:
From downtown Cincinnati, follow Central Parkway as it winds northward. Drive approximately 1.6 miles and turn right on W. McMillan Ave. Cross McMicken Ave. and watch for the Park's entrance on your right as you snake up the ridge. Park along this drive, near the playground (see map).

Route:
After enjoying the spectacular view of downtown Cincinnati, walk east along the Park's roadway. Turn left on Ravine St., one of our city's steepest streets. Walk ½ block and turn left along Warner St., ascending further up the ridge. At the top of the hill walk 1 block to another overlook of the Cincinnati basin.

Walk north along Fairview Ave. which eventually curves to the right and intersects McMillan Ave. **St. Monica's Church,** on your right, was completed in 1927. Constructed with Indiana limestone, the Church's 130 ft. tower is visible across much of the lower Mill Creek Valley. The building's interior is adorned with stained glass and paintings from Munich, Germany. St. Monica Church served as the regional Catholic cathedral during the renovation of St. Peter in Chains (1938-1957).

Cross McMillan Ave. and turn left along this heavily traveled road. Wind downhill and re-cross McMillan at the Park's entrance. Follow Scenic Drive which hugs the hillside and offers constant views to the south and west. Returning to your car, your walk through Fairview Park and Clifton Heights has totalled 1.7 miles.

View of the Mill Creek Valley

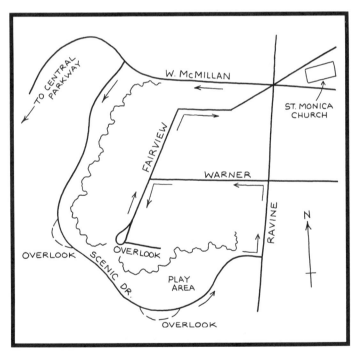

FAIRVIEW PARK/CLIFTON HEIGHTS

36 OVER-THE-RHINE/LIBERTY HILL

Distance: 1.2 miles
Terrain: hilly; steep areas

During the mid 1800s, German immigrants, attracted to Cincinnati by its
booming economy, settled the area north
of the Miami-Erie Canal, an area they
nostalgically called "**Over-the-Rhine.**"
Unfortunately, a century later, this section
of town began to decay as its middle
class citizens departed for outlying
neighborhoods. Its attractive brick homes,
abandoned to the poor and dispossessed,
started to crumble and the area became
little more than a sprawling slum. Only a
few businesses remained to preserve the
German heritage of this once thriving
community.

During the 1960s, an infusion of Federal
funds initiated an effort to rejuvenate this
historic district. However, the movement
stalled until urban renewal became a
political and economic necessity during
the late 1970s and early 1980s. Most of the
area's renovation is clustered near the
northernmost blocks of Sycamore Street.

Directions:

For a 1.2 mile walking tour of this
revived neighborhood, park in one of the
lots along Sycamore St., between 11th and
13th Streets.

Route:

Walk northward along Sycamore. **The
Diner (1)**, a popular bar and restaurant,
opened in April, 1984. It is built around an
authentic Mountainview Dining Car,
constructed in 1955. The car was used in
Massilon, Ohio, until it was moved to
Cincinnati in 1984.

On the northeast corner of 13th and
Sycamore is the **School for Creative &
Performing Arts (2)**. Opened in 1977, the
School occupies the old Woodward High
School building which was constructed in
1910. Woodward High was established on

this site in 1831, the first public high school
west of the Appalachians. Named for its
founder, surveyor and real estate magnate
William Woodward, the school moved to its
present-day location, at Seymour Avenue
and Reading Road, in 1953.

Continuing north along Sycamore you
will soon pass **Salem's Kirche (3)**. This
Gothic Revival structure, now the Salem
United Church of Christ, was completed in
1867; the Church is home to Gabriel's
Corner, a community arts center. Cross
Liberty St. and ascend the hill for two
blocks. Turn right along Boal St.; after
walking 1½ blocks you will reach a **small
park (4)** which offers a spectacular view of
downtown Cincinnati. Descend through
the park and turn left along Milton St. This
appealing avenue is lined with renovated
homes, most of which possess fine views of
the city.

At the end of Milton, turn right along
Highland Avenue, crossing to its east side
for a broad view of the I-71 corridor. Eden
Park and Mt. Adams rise beyond the
highway. To the south are views of the
P&G Towers, the I-471 bridge and the
Northern Kentucky hills.

Curving to the right, Highland Avenue
becomes Liberty Hill and descends to
Liberty St. Cross Liberty at Broadway
and walk southward past two blocks of
revitalized rowhouses. Turn left at 12th St.
and ascend to **St. Paul's Church (5)**.
Completed in 1850, the Romanesque
Church and its adjacent buildings have
been renovated and are now the home of
Pendleton Square, a design center. Just
east of the Church building is **St. Paul's
School (6)**, which opened as a boys school
in 1862; the structure became a girls school
in 1908.

Descend to Reading Road, turn right and
proceed two blocks to Sycamore. Turn
right and return to your car, completing a
1.2 mile walk.

Rowhouses along Milton St.

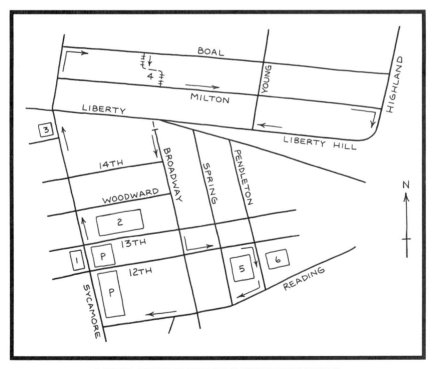

OVER-THE-RHINE/LIBERTY HILL

37 PLUM ST./CENTRAL PARKWAY/EIGHTH ST.

Distance: 1.8 miles
Terrain: flat

If you don't mind mixing religion and politics, the following walk will take you past some of Cincinnati's most impressive buildings.

Directions:
Park in one of the decks at 6th & Elm Sts., near the western edge of downtown Cincinnati (see map).

Route:
Walk northward along Elm St. The **Cincinnati Bell Telephone Building (1)** fills the southwest corner of 7th and Elm Sts. Established in 1878, the Company moved to this magnificent building in the early 1900s. Continue along Elm to the **Covenant First Presbyterian Church (2)**, at 8th and Elm. Dedicated in 1875, this Church's congregation is a composite of four Presbyterian communities, the oldest of which dates back to 1790.

Turn left on 8th St. and proceed one block to Plum. This is surely the most powerful intersection in Cincinnati. On the southeast corner is the **Plum St. Temple (3)**. The Temple was constructed in 1866 and provides an excellent example of Moorish Revival architecture. Under the leadership of Rabbi Isaac M. Wise, it was the site of the first ordination of rabbis in America.

On the southwest corner of 8th and Plum is **St. Peter in Chains Cathedral (4)**, completed in 1845. Its 200 foot steeple is visible throughout much of the Cincinnati basin. The Cathedral, spiritual center of our city's Roman Catholic community, was closed for renovation from 1938 to 1957. St. Monica Church, in Clifton Heights, served as the temporary cathedral during that time.

Cincinnati's City Hall (5), looms above the northwest corner of 8th & Plum. Dating from 1892, this Romanesque building's fine, red granite stone work was supervised by David Hummel, who also built Scarlet Oaks (in Clifton) and the Eden Park Water Tower.

Walk north along Plum St. which soon merges into **Central Parkway**. This wide boulevard, completed in 1926, covers the channel of the old **Miami-Erie Canal** and Cincinnati's ill-fated subway line. The Cincinnati-Dayton section of the Canal opened in 1827 but closed by the early 1900s. Plans were then advanced to construct a subway through the old Canal bed. The futile work began in 1920 and the project was abandoned soon thereafter. Remnants of the subway still remain beneath the Parkway today.

Continue northward along Central Parkway for two blocks and turn right on 12th St. On the northwest corner of 12th and Elm is the **Apostolic Bethlehem Temple (6)**. This structure was originally the St. John Unitarian Church, the first German-Protestant congregation in Cincinnati. Turn left along Elm St. **Memorial Hall (7)** is a fine example of Beaux-Arts Classical Revival architecture. Completed in 1908 and designed by Samuel Hannaford & Sons, the building was dedicated to pioneers and soldiers. Over the past 85 years it has been used for community meetings, concerts, graduation ceremonies and other cultural events. It is now home to the Cincinnati Preservation Association and is listed on the National Register of Historic Places. Formerly known as the Miami Purchase Association and founded in 1964, the **Cincinnati Preservation Association** directs the protection and preservation of historic structures, neighborhoods and archaeological sites throughout the Tristate region; for more information, contact them at the address/phone listed in Appendix II.

Looking north down Plum St.

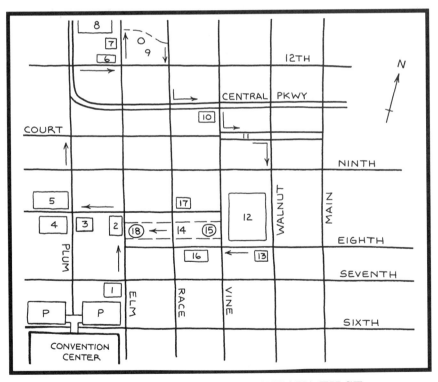

PLUM ST./CENTRAL PARKWAY/8TH ST.

Continue along Elm St. to the grand entrance of Cincinnati's famed **Music Hall (8)**. Designed by Samuel Hannaford, perhaps our city's most renowned architect, this palatial building opened in 1878. Its construction was spear-headed by Reuben Springer whose statue graces the Hall's foyer. Springer saw the need for a spacious concert hall where the German community could enjoy their regular music programs, especially the May Festivals. First held in 1873, the Festival remains the oldest annual choral festival in the Americas.

Backtrack along Elm St. for ½ block and cut through **Washington Park (9)**. Centered around a gazebo/bandstand, this urban park, acquired by Cincinnati in 1855, was initially the site of a Presbyterian cemetery. Walk south along Race St., turn left on Central Parkway and then right along Vine St. The **Cincinnatus Building (10)**, adorned with a spectacular mural of the Roman soldier after whom our city was named, was formerly the Brotherhood Building. The renovated building and its fabulous mural were dedicated in July, 1983, in celebration of the 100th Anniversary of the Kroger Company. Proceed one block and turn left, passing through **Court Street Marketplace (11)**.

Turn right on Walnut St. **Library Square (12)** fills the block between 8th & 9th Sts. The Public Library of Cincinnati & Hamilton County moved to this location in 1955 (it formerly occupied the building at 617 Vine). The Library underwent extensive renovation and expansion during the early 1980s and is now one of the most impressive public libraries in the country. Established in 1867, the central library coordinates branch facilities throughout Hamilton County.

St. Louis Catholic Church (13) sits on the southwest corner of 8th and Walnut. This limestone building, Florentine in style, was dedicated in 1930. Walk westward along 8th St., crossing Vine, and enter **Piatt Park (14)**. Donated to the city by John and Benjamin Piatt in 1817, the Park stretches between Vine and Elm. A bronze **statue of President James Garfield (15)**, unveiled in 1887, graces the east end of the Park. The **Presidential Plaza (16)**, formerly the Doctor's Building, was recently renovated. Built in 1923, this Gothic Revival structure was added to the National Register of Historic Places in 1987. North of the Park is the **Cincinnati Club (17)**; this impressive limestone building was completed in 1924. A **statue of William Henry Harrison (18)**, on horseback, stands at the west end of Piatt Park. Dedicated in 1896, the statue emphasizes Harrison's long military service that preceeded his political career.

Turn left (south) along Elm St. and return to the parking decks. Your walking tour has totalled 1.8 miles.

Music Hall from Washington Park

Garfield Statue at Piatt Park

38 SKYWALK/FOUNTAIN SQUARE/FIFTH ST.

Distance: 2.0 miles
Terrain: flat; some stairways

Cincinnati's extensive skywalk system, often praised by urban planning groups, debuted in 1972. This elevated walkway links many of the downtown buildings while providing an escape from the noise and congestion of city traffic. Along its route are many of Cincinnati's luxury hotels and several of her most famous landmarks.

Directions:

Park in one of the decks at 6th and Elm, near the western edge of downtown Cincinnati.

Route:

The skywalk begins between the parking decks along 6th Street (see map), where an **iron bell (1)**, struck at the Buckeye Bell Foundry in 1885, commemorates the site of an Open Market which served the community through much of the 1800s. Cross over 6th St. and enter the **Convention Center (2)**.

Initially opened in 1967, the Center was expanded and renovated in the mid 1980s to keep up with the city's thriving convention business. The present-day 165,000 square-foot complex, dedicated in 1987, was renamed in honor of Dr. Albert B. Sabin who developed the oral polio vaccine. Walk southward through the Center and turn left at the end of the hall, soon reaching the entry plaza at 5th and Elm. Descend to the next level and cross over 5th St. to **Convention Place Mall (3)**, home to a gallery of specialty shops.

Follow the walkway eastward, crossing Elm and entering the **Hyatt Hotel (4)**. The Hotel's large, sun-lit piano lounge always invites a stop for refreshment. Adjacent to the Hyatt is **Saks Fifth Avenue (5)**. Cross over Race St. and descend to the Carew Tower Arcade which stretches below

Cincinnati's tallest building. Rising 48 stories, the **Carew Tower (6)** yields a spectacular view of the Ohio and Mill Creek Valleys from its lofty observation deck. The Tower was completed in 1930 and its street-level Arcade, lined with shops, soda fountains and restaurants, retains the flavor of the early 20th Century.

Ascend back to the skywalk, re-cross Race St. and turn left. A third crossing of Race St. takes you into **Tower Place (7)**, a fine collection of upscale shops that opened in 1990. After circling the inner atrium of Tower Place, the skywalk angles northeastward and soon crosses Vine St., entering the **Westin Hotel (8)**. Always bustling with activity, the Hotel opened in 1981. Its large atrium is often the site of cultural and holiday displays.

Cross over 5th St. on the Skywalk extension that leads out to **Fountain Square (9)**. Enlarged and remodeled in the 1960s, the Square is the site of free concerts, street fairs, political demonstrations and general relaxation throughout the year. Its most striking feature is the **Tyler Davidson Fountain (10)**, Cincinnati's famous landmark. Purchased in Bavaria, the Fountain was a gift to the people of Cincinnati from Henry Probasco; it was dedicated in 1871 and named in honor of Mr. Probasco's brother-in-law.

Walk eastward along Fifth St. The **U.S. Post Office Building (11)**, completed in 1939, fills the next block north of Fifth. Beyond Walnut St. are the **Federal Building (12)** and the **Chiquita Center (13)**. The latter, which opened in 1983, is topped by a "weather beacon," the color of which indicates the next day's forecast. The **Chemed Center (14)**, across Fifth St., is one of many new office towers to rise in downtown Cincinnati during the late 1980s.

Fountain Square

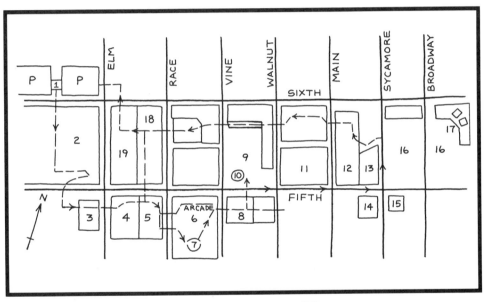

SKYWALK/FIFTH ST.

East of the Chemed Center is the **Taft Theater (15),** which opened in 1928. This 2500 seat theater, the site of Broadway productions throughout the year, was designed by Henry Hake and was named for Charles P. Taft, Cincinnati's famous philanthropist.

Turn left on Sycamore Street. Across Sycamore, the **Procter & Gamble Plaza (16)** sweeps toward the company's **twin-tower office complex (17),** which was completed in 1985. Pick up the Skywalk behind the Chiquita Center (see map) and head westward. After cutting through office towers, skirting Fountain Square and crossing four streets, the Skywalk enters the **Fifth & Race Tower Arcade (18)** and the **Clarion Hotel (19).** Angle right at the Clarion, crossing 6th Street and Elm Street to enter the parking garage. Your walking tour of Cincinnati's central business district has totalled 2 miles.

39 CINCINNATI RIVERFRONT/ LYTLE PARK HISTORIC DISTRICT

Distance: 2.6 miles
Terrain: mostly flat; few stairways

This walking tour of **Cincinnati's Riverfront** and the **Lytle Park Historic District** starts where our city began, at the **Public Landing (1)** along the banks of the Ohio. It was in this area that the first boat of settlers came ashore on December 28, 1788. They called their pioneer town "Losantiville", meaning "the village across from the mouth of the Licking River." As the city grew, the Public Landing became the hub of a thriving steamboat port. While most of the "tall stacks" have long since disappeared, Cincinnati's Delta Queen and the **Showboat Majestic (2)** still dock along this shore. The latter, built in 1923, is a permanent feature of the Landing and is used for theater productions. Acquired by the city in 1967, the Showboat was added to the National Registry of Historic Places in 1980.

Directions:

Leave your car at the Public Landing which stretches along the the Ohio River at the foot of Broadway.

Route:

Walk eastward, entering **Yeatman's Cove Park (3)**. Opened in 1976, the Park is named for Griffin Yeatman who operated the "Square & Compass" tavern near this site back in the 1790's. A unique feature of the Park is the **Serpentine Wall (4)**, a contoured, concrete wall of steps, used for concerts and river watching. The Park itself is a popular spot for picnic lunches and is regularly used for festivals throughout the warmer months. Along the north edge of the Park is the **Lytle Place Fountain (5)** and wading area, a cool retreat on hot summer days.

Proceed eastward through the bricked "**Skyline Arches**" (6) beneath the L&N

Bridge. Entering the "**Bicentennial Commons at Sawyer Point**" (7), you are greeted by a 12-foot **statue of Cincinnatus (8)**, the Roman soldier and farmer after whom our city was named. The 22-acre Park opened in June, 1988, in celebration of Cincinnati's Bicentennial. Bear left along the north edge of the central lawn. The **P&G Pavilion (9)** is used for concerts and other performances during the warmer months of the year.

North of the Pavilion area is the main entrance to Bicentennial Commons. This includes the famous "**flying pig sculptures**" (10) and a **flowing model of the Ohio River and its numerous locks (11)**. The **Bicentennial Brick Promenade (12)** stretches along the southern rim of the entry complex. Sponsored by the Kroger Co., this path of bricks, each imprinted with the name of a Tristate resident or family, created the opportunity to both fund the Park and purchase a "place" in the history of our city.

Continue eastward past the **Fitness Area (13), Playground (14), volleyball courts (15), Lindner Tennis Complex (16)**, the **Schott Amphitheater (17)**, all-weather **skating rink (18)** and the **Boathouse (19)**. The latter houses a restaurant and an Olympic rowing center. The Schott Amphitheater preserves a section of Cincinnati's old waterworks plant.

Return along the walkway that parallels the riverbank (see map). Several overlooks and a **fishing pier (20)** jut over the water, providing views of the Ohio River and Northern Kentucky's hills. Pass through the **Skyline Arches (6)** and continue westward through Yeatman's Cove Park. Angle north to the **Lytle Place Fountain (5)** and ascend the stairs to the **pedestrian bridge (21)** that crosses over Ft. Washington Way.

Riverboats at Yeatman's Cove Park

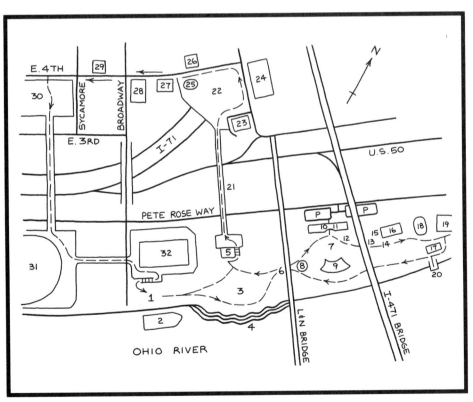

CINCINNATI RIVERFRONT/LYTLE PARK DISTRICT

Just north of the highway is **Lytle Park (22)**, a beautiful, green oasis, purchased by the city in 1905. Spectacular floral displays adorn the park from April to October and shaded benches entice visitors during the heat of summer. On the southeast edge of the Park is the **Anna Louise Inn (23)**, a residence and social center for young women since 1909. The Inn is named for the daughter of Charles P. Taft. At the east end of the Park is the **Taft Museum (24)**. Built in 1820 by Martin Baum, a local banker and manufacturer, the house was later occupied by Nicholas Longworth, whose vineyards cloaked the Mt. Adams ridge. Charles P. Taft purchased the home in 1900 and it was here that William Howard Taft accepted the Republican nomination for President in 1908. Charles Taft donated the house to the city of Cincinnati in 1932.

Near the west end of Lytle Park is a **statue of President Abraham Lincoln (25)**, dedicated in 1917. It was yet another gift to the city from the Charles P. Taft family. Along the north edge of the Park, at 500 E. 4th St., is **The Literary Club (26)**. Completed in 1820, this building provides an excellent example of Georgian style architecture. The Literary Club, established in 1849, moved to this site in 1875.

Walk west along E. 4th St. A plaque on the **Guilford School building (27)** commemorates the site of Fort Washington, a federal outpost that was instrumental in the early development of our city. The **University Club building (28)**, at 4th and Broadway, dates from 1880. The Club itself was founded in 1879 and moved to this location in 1907.

Cross Broadway and continue west. **Christ Episcopal Church (29)**, at 318 E. 4th St., was completed in 1835. Cross Sycamore St., continue ½ block and turn left into the **Atrium I Building (30)**, just opposite the "Skywalk" sign. Cut through the center's attractive atrium and follow the walkway that crosses Ft. Washington Way (see map). Along the way, a history of baseball is presented via a series of overhead posters.

The walkway leads onto the plaza surrounding **Riverfront Stadium (31)**. Home to the Reds and Bengals, the stadium opened on June 30, 1970. Turn left across the bridge that connects the stadium plaza with the **Riverfront Coliseum complex (32)**. The Coliseum opened in September, 1975 and seats up to 17,800 spectators.

Descend to the Public Landing from the south side of Riverfront Coliseum (see map). Your tour of the city's riverside parks and historic Lytle Park District has totalled 2.6 miles.

The Taft Museum

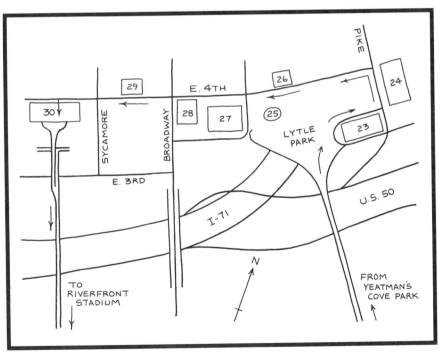

E. FOURTH ST./LYTLE PARK

40 EDEN PARK

Distance: 2.8 miles
Terrain: rolling; few steep areas

When Nicholas Longworth, one of Cincinnati's early land barons, planted his vineyards across the flanks of Mt. Ida, little did he know that his "Garden of Eden" would someday become one of America's premier municipal parks. Established in 1859, **Eden Park** spreads for 184 acres along this wooded ridge. A beautiful refuge for city dwellers, it is also home to several of Cincinnati's finest cultural attractions.

Directions:

From downtown Cincinnati, head east on Columbia Parkway (U.S. 50). After passing I-471, stay to the right and exit onto the narrow, concrete viaduct that circles back across the Parkway. At the stop sign, turn right on Martin Drive and follow this road until it deadends into Eden Park Drive. Turn right, pass under the bridge and turn left on St. Paul Place. Park along this drive, across from the red-brick **Water Tower (1)**.

Route:

The **Water Tower**, rising 172 feet, is visible throughout much of the Cincinnati area. It was constructed in 1894, to improve water flow to Walnut Hills. No longer used as a storage reservoir, the structure remains one of our most attractive and recognizable landmarks.

Before walking across the bridge, descend the slope to the **Vietnam Memorial (2)**. Dedicated on April 8, 1984, the monument was designed by Ken Bradford and sculpted by Eleftherious Karkadoulious, who also restored the Tyler Davidson and President Garfield statues downtown.

Cross the concrete arch bridge and stop at the **Eden Park Overlook (3)**, which offers a spectacular view of the Ohio River Valley. Dayton and Bellevue, Kentucky, are directly across the River and Ft. Thomas

sprawls along the southern horizon. The Overlook's granite obelisk commemorates the canalization of the Ohio and marks the River's halfway point. The monument was dedicated by President Hoover in 1929.

Walk westward for about 100 feet and descend the stairs that lead to the **Krohn Conservatory (4)**. Housing a vast array of plant life, from tropical palms to desert cacti, the Conservatory is open to the public throughout the year. Its warm confines and colorful flowers are especially inviting on a cold winter day.

Beyond the Conservatory a walkway crosses Martin Drive and heads westward, paralleling Eden Park Drive (see map). This route winds across an open garden, through a natural woodland and onto the lawn that surrounds **Eden Park's reflecting pool (5)**. At the northwest corner of the lawn is perhaps the most photographed landmark in Cincinnati's Park system...the **Spring-House**. This **gazebo (6)** was initially built in 1905 to cover a natural spring. It now provides a shady rest-stop for park visitors.

Ascend from this basin, following Art Museum Drive (see map). You will soon pass the **Bandstand (7)**, set in a natural amphitheater, where concerts and plays are often held during the warmer months. The present Bandstand was constructed in 1915, replacing the former 1872 structure.

Bear right at the top of the ridge for a walk past the hub of Cincinnati's art community... the **Art Academy (8)** and **Art Museum (9)**. The Cincinnati Art Academy, founded in 1869, moved to Eden Park in 1887, where Frank Duveneck was its dean from 1888 to 1919. The Museum's central, limestone building was opened in 1886; several wings were added during the early 1900's.

Head back across the ridge and ascend further to Mt. Adams Drive, which loops around the **Playhouse in the Park (10)**. Operated by the Tristate's only nonprofit,

The Krohn Conservatory

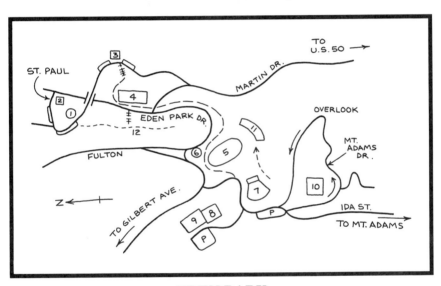

EDEN PARK

professional Theater company, the Playhouse first opened in 1960. The original Thompson Shelterhouse Theater seats 220 persons while the Robert S. Marx Theater, added in 1968, seats 629. The Playhouse's eleven-production season, which runs from September to August, is funded through the Fine Arts Fund, the Ohio Arts Council and the National Endowment for the Arts.

An overlook at the south end of Mt. Adams Drive offers another view of the Ohio Valley. Continue around this road and descend along the path that cuts past the Bandstand (see map) and leads onto the reflecting pool lawn. Stop by the **retaining wall (11),** part of Cincinnati's old reservoir system, for yet another expansive view to the south.

Re-trace your initial route to **Krohn Conservatory (4)** and cross Eden Park Drive, ascending a stairway to the **Presidential Grove (12).** Here trees have been planted to honor each U.S. President, starting with the George Washington oak, in 1882.

Walk north along the ridge, returning to your car. Your tour of Nicholas Longworth's "Garden of Eden" has totalled 2.8 miles.

41 MT. ADAMS

Distance: 1.4 miles
Terrain: steep hills

To Cincinnatians, "Mt. Adams" brings to mind steep, narrow streets, broad vistas, outdoor cafes and quaint shops. Indeed, perched high above the city's basin, **Mt. Adams** is one of the more unique communities in our metropolitan area. A walk through its hilly maze offers a pleasing blend of history and modern leisure.

Directions:

Follow Gilbert Ave. north and east from the downtown area (this avenue is the eastern extension of 7th St.) Drive approximately 1 mile and turn right on Eden Park Drive. Bear right onto Art Museum Drive and park in the gravel lot at the top of the ridge (see map).

Route:

Walk south along Ida St. Mt. Adams was originally called "Mt. Ida" and was the site of Nicholas Longworth's extensive vineyard. The ridge was renamed "Mt. Adams" in 1843, honoring President John Quincy Adams who visited Cincinnati to dedicate the city's original Observatory.

After walking 1 block you will come to the **Ida St. bridge (1)** which yields an expansive view of the lower Mill Creek Valley to the west. Completed in 1931, the current reinforced concrete bridge replaced an older wooden structure. At the north end of the bridge is the **Pilgrim Presbyterian Church (2)**, dating from 1887.

Beyond the bridge is the **Rookwood Pottery Building (3)**. Formerly a bustling pottery works, which moved to Mt. Adams in 1892, the structure now houses an appealing restaurant and bar. Walk to the back of the parking lot between **Rookwood** and **the Celestial Tower (4)** for a spectacular view of downtown Cincinnati and the Riverfront Area.

Across from the Celestial Tower is a **plaque (5)** that briefly describes the history of this hilltop community. Backtrack along Ida St. for ½ block and turn right on Monastery St., ascending a steep hill. Turn right along St. Paul St. for a short walk past the grounds of the **Holy Cross Monastery (6)**. Completed in 1899, the Monastery occupies the original site of the Cincinnati Observatory. The latter was moved to its current location, in Mt. Lookout, in 1875.

Descend along Pavilion St. (see map), cross over St. Gregory St. and continue east for 1½ blocks. Turn right along the driveway that leads back to the **Church of the Immaculate Conception (7)**. Built in 1862, this prominent Cincinnati landmark is a Good Friday pilgrimage site for Tristate Catholics. From its portico one has a sweeping view of the Ohio Valley, Northern Kentucky and the Cincinnati basin.

Descend the **stairway (8)** to St. Gregory St. Turn right and follow this street through the central village area. St. Gregory is the "Main St." of Mt. Adams and many of the area's most popular cafes and nightclubs are clustered near its course. One of these, **Longworth's Restaurant (9)**, occupies an old firehouse that was built in 1887.

At the north end of St. Gregory St., turn right for ½ block and then left on Louden St. Walk 1 block and turn left, following Paradrome St. and Mt. Adams Drive back to Ida St. (see map). **Cincinnati's Playhouse in the Park (10)** sits on a wooded hill to your right. Opened in 1960, the Playhouse will celebrate the start of its 30th season in September, 1989. For more on the Playhouse see the Eden Park tour.

Return to your car via Ida St. Your roller coaster stroll through Mt. Adams has totalled 1.4 miles.

A view to the west

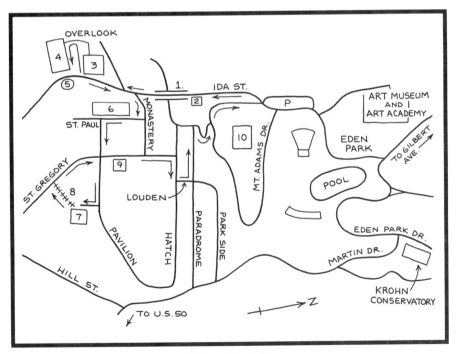

MT. ADAMS

42 ALMS PARK/MT. LOOKOUT/TUSCULUM

Distance: 4.6 miles
Terrain: hilly; steep areas

Alms Park, perched on a ridge above the junction of the Little Miami and Ohio River Valleys, is a terrific spot for a picnic. We suggest combining your picnic lunch with a pleasant hike through the adjacent neighborhoods of **Mt. Lookout.**

This area of Cincinnati was initially known as Spencer Township. Annexed by the city in 1870, it was renamed **Mt. Lookout** in 1875 when Cincinnati's Observatory was moved to the area from Mt. Adams. Today, the neighborhood's winding streets, shaded lots and attractive homes have drawn a new influx of residents. Modern houses hug the ridgetops, offering spectacular views, while older avenues, lined with stately homes, radiate from the central square.

Directions:

To reach the area from downtown Cincinnati, follow Columbia Parkway (U.S. 50) east. Drive approximately 4.2 miles and turn left on Delta Ave. Ascend the hill for 1 mile and park in or near Mt. Lookout Square, formed by the intersection of Delta and Linwood Avenues.

Route:

Walk east along Linwood Ave., ascending a gentle hill. After hiking three blocks, turn right on Tweed Ave., following this road until it ends. Turn right on Kroger Ave. for ½ block and then left on Stanley Ave. Cross over Grandin Rd., continue for 1 block and turn left onto Vineyard Place. From this point to the Park, the route is devoid of sidewalks and, since the roads are winding and narrow, caution is advised. Vineyard Place curves along a ridgetop, its new homes endowed with superb views of the Ohio Valley.

Turn right on Tusculum Ave., descending for about ¼ mile to the Park's entrance (see

map). The site of **Alms Park** was once known as Bald Knob, reflecting the fact that local Indians had cleared the summit for purposes of a lookout. The area was later called Tusculum Heights since it overlooked the riverside town of Tusculum. The Park itself, covering 85 acres, was donated to Cincinnati by Mrs. Frederick Alms in 1916, as a memorial to her late husband.

Follow the Park road, bearing right along the loop (see map). You will soon arrive at the **Stephen Foster Memorial (1).** This bronze statue, dedicated in 1937, commemorates the famous songwriter who spent several years in Cincinnati.

Proceed to the **Park's Pavilion (2).** From its upper portico one has a broad view of the Ohio Valley, backed by the Kentucky hills. The Park's east **overlook (3)** offers a spectacular view of the Little Miami Valley, including Lunken Airport. Children especially enjoy this panorama, entertained by the planes and helicopters that zoom across the valley. North of the Airport, the Little Miami Valley cuts into the southern Ohio countryside. Directly east, Mt. Washington stretches across the scene while the Ohio River curves in from the southeast, its waters often dotted with pleasure boats. The I-275 bridge spans the River, approximately 2 miles upstream from the Airport.

Complete the Park loop and turn left on Tusculum, descending toward the Ohio River. You will soon reach the old community of **Tusculum,** founded in 1788, where colorful, Victorian homes are clustered across the hillside.

Turn right on Columbia Parkway and then right along Stanley Avenue, enduring a long, steady climb onto the ridge. Return to Mt. Lookout Square by turning left on

Victorian homes along Tusculum

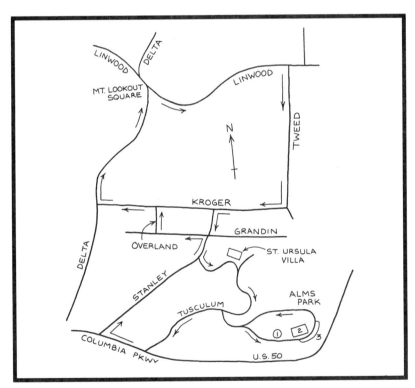

ALMS PARK/MT. LOOKOUT/TUSCULUM

Grandin, right on Overland, left on Kroger and right on Delta (see map). Celebrate! Your roundtrip journey has totalled 4.6 miles (and you've likely burned off that picnic lunch).

43 LUNKEN AIRPORT

Hike Bike Trail
Distance: 6.2 miles
Terrain: flat

When **Lunken Airport** was dedicated in 1932, it was the largest municipal airport in the United States. However, in the decades following the opening of the Boone County Airport (now Greater Cincinnati/ Northern Kentucky International Airport), Lunken, the original home of American Airlines, reverted to a set of sleepy runways in the lowlands of eastern Hamilton County. Visitors would stop by to watch an occasional piper cub drift in along the Little Miami Valley.

With increasing traffic at Cincinnati/ Northern Kentucky International, growing interest in private aviation, improved flood control and the arrival of the corporate jet age, Lunken Airport has experienced a renewal in the 1980's. This resurgence of aviation has been matched by an influx of joggers, walkers and cyclists to the Airport's flatlands.

Directions:

To reach Lunken Airport from downtown Cincinnati, follow Columbia Parkway (U.S. 50 east) for approximately 4.5 miles. Turn right on Stanley Ave., drive two blocks and turn left on Kellogg Ave. (U.S. 52). Drive approximately 1 mile and turn left on Wilmer Ave. Park along Airport Rd. or at the playground, north of Lunken (see map).

If possible, plan a weekday visit to avoid the weekend crush of joggers and cyclists. In addition, due to the open, flat terrain and funneling effect of adjacent ridges, be advised that the wind-chill factor can be severe during the colder months.

Route:

A 6.2 mile **Hike/Bike Trail** loops around the airfield. Access to the trail is provided by parking areas along Airport Rd. or at the playground, north of Lunken (see map). The western rim of the loop parallels Wilmer Ave. while its eastern and southern sections run atop flood control levees. These elevated pathways offer broad views of the Airport and surrounding hills. In addition, the levees are flanked by thickets and woodlands, providing an excellent avenue for birdwatching. Indeed, veteran birders flock to Lunken each winter to look for short-eared owls, which arrive from Canada to hunt on the valley's grasslands.

Of historical interest is **Pioneer Cemetery**, located along Wilmer Ave., 1 block north of Airport Rd. (see map). This small plot contains the graves of Major Benjamin Stites and the other New Jersey citizens who founded the settlement of **Columbia** here in November, 1788. Their town predated Losantiville (Cincinnati) by 1 month.

Attracted to the area by the fertile "Turkey Bottoms" of the Little Miami floodplain, the settlers clustered their log homes near a stockade for protection from regional Indians. They erected the Northwest Territory's first Protestant church, in 1790.

The **ornate column (1)** at the top of the cemetery steps honors "The first boat load" of settlers who now lie beneath weathered limestone markers. **Major Benjamin Stites' gravestone (2)** was replaced in November 1923, at a ceremony commemorating the 135th anniversary of Columbia's founding.

Lunken Airport from Alms Park

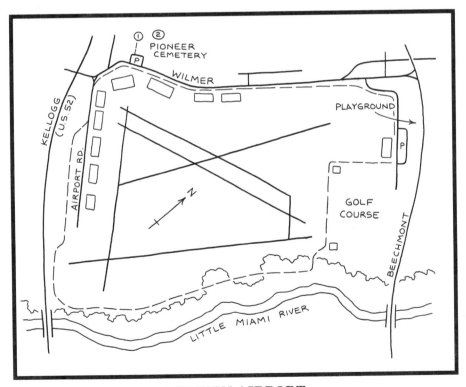

LUNKEN AIRPORT

44 MAGRISH RIVERLANDS PRESERVE

Distance: 1.2 mile loop
Terrain: flat; few stairways

Wetlands and riparian forest have long been among the most threatened ecosystems on our planet. Waterways are dammed, marshes are drained, groundwater is polluted and stream banks are used as dumping grounds. Only through the persistent efforts of dedicated individuals and conservation organizations have some wetlands been protected from these destructive forces.

Such is the case at **Magrish Riverlands Preserve** along the east bank of the Little Miami River. The effort to protect this floodplain refuge has been ongoing for over twenty years. Prompted by the donation of land and funds to the city of Cincinnati by Edith Magrish, in memory of her husband James, the Cincinnati Recreation Commission has directed cleanup of the site and is now working to improve access to the Preserve.

The Magrish Riverlands are characterized by marsh, wet meadows and riparian woodlands, stretching along the east bank of the Little Miami near its confluence with the Ohio River. Seasonal flooding has discouraged the "development" of this land but easements for the dumping of dredge mud from nearby harbors are still in effect. Nevertheless, a visit to the Preserve yields a fine introduction to the flora and fauna of these riverside habitats.

Directions:

From Downtown Cincinnati, follow U.S. 50 (Columbia Parkway) east. Drive approximately 4.5 miles and turn right on Stanley Avenue. Proceed 2 blocks and turn left on U.S. 52 (Kellogg Ave.). Drive another 2 miles and exit onto Salem Road; after crossing over Kellogg Avenue the Preserve entrance will be a short distance, on your left (see map).

Alternatively, from I-275 east of Cincinnati, take Exit #72 and head west on Kellogg Avenue. Drive 1.6 miles to Salem Road and turn right: the Preserve will be a short distance on your left.

Route:

The trail network at Magrish Riverlands Preserve was still being developed when we visited the refuge in 1993. However, we reviewed future plans with Jim Farfsing, Coordinator of Outdoor Education for the Cincinnati Recreation Commission, and the map in this guide should serve as a reliable illustration of the primary routes.

From the parking area, pick up the trail that curves westward and then northward, paralleling the major roadways (see map). This path circles the primary marshland, eventually crossing the drainage stream near the south bank of the Little Miami. During the warmer months, watch for common yellowthroats, willow flycatchers, yellow warblers and gray catbirds in the moist thickets. Green-backed and great blue herons may stop to fish the shallows, joined by black-crowned night herons at dusk. Song sparrows, red-winged blackbirds, mallards and belted kingfishers are year-round residents of the Preserve.

Turn eastward above the Little Miami, stopping by the overlook (V) for a broad view of this scenic River. Descend a stairway and enter the floodplain forest; water-loving trees such as sycamore, maple, hackberry, and river birch are the predominant species. Bear left onto the trail that winds eastward above the riverbank, bypassing side trails that cut to the south. The main route eventually curves away from the River and intersects a power line swath. Turn right and return to the parking area via this wide path.

A riparian woodland borders the Little Miami River

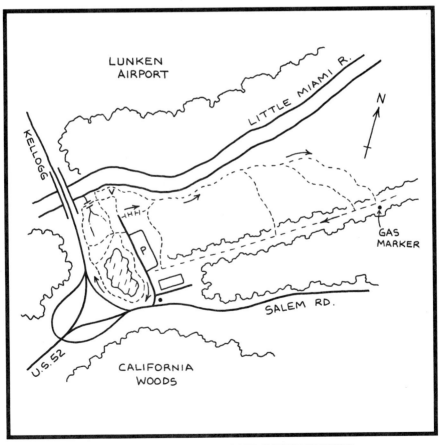

LUNKEN AIRPORT

LITTLE MIAMI R.

KELLOGG

N

P

GAS MARKER

U.S. 52

SALEM RD.

CALIFORNIA WOODS

MAGRISH RIVERLANDS PRESERVE

45 CALIFORNIA WOODS NATURE PRESERVE

California Junction Trail
Distance: 1.25 miles
Terrain: hilly

Meadow Loop
Distance: 1.5 miles
Terrain: hilly

Combined Loop Hike
Distance: 2.0 miles
Terrain: hilly; steep areas

California Woods Nature Preserve is draped over two parallel ridges near the mouth of the Little Miami River. Established in 1937 and managed by the Cincinnati Recreation Commission, the Preserve's 110 acres are cloaked with a mature beech-maple forest. Huge sycamores rise along the creek beds and tulip trees speckle the woodland. Forest wildflowers are abundant in spring and birdwatching is excellent here throughout the year.

A network of eleven trails provides access to the Preserve. Two of these, the **California Junction Trail (CJT)** and the **Trillium Valley Trail (TVT)**, are National Recreation Trails.

Directions:

The entrance to California Woods Nature Preserve is off Kellogg Avenue (U.S. 52), .5 mile east of the Little Miami River. From I-275 on the east side of Greater Cincinnati, take Exit #72 and head west on Kellogg Avenue. The Preserve entrance will be 1.1 miles ahead, on your right.

Park in the small gravel lot along the left side of the entry road (see map); a nominal day-use fee is charged. Pets are **not** permitted at California Woods Nature Preserve.

Routes:

For an overview of California Woods we recommend the following trail loops.

California Junction Trail (CJT; 1.25 miles). Dedicated as a National Recreation Trail in October, 1988, this loop begins along the entry road, approximately 50 yards west of the parking lot (see map). It first skirts a creek bed and then ascends the ridge via a series of earthen steps. At the top of the hill, turn right along a straight, level section of the trail. You are following the old bed of the Cincinnati Georgetown & Portsmouth Railroad. Opened in 1878, the rail line shut down during the great flood of 1937. California Woods was the "junction" where a side track angled off to Coney Island.

At the north end of the loop the trail passes through a shelter house, veers to the left and descends onto the Little Miami floodplain. Paralleling Kellogg Avenue, the trail crosses several small streams and gradually ascends along the southern flank of the ridge. After rejoining the old railroad bed, evidenced by the levee-like topography, complete the loop and return to your car via the entry path.

Combined Loop Hike (2.0 miles). Pick up the **Trillium Valley Trail (TVT)** just west of the parking lot. Another National Recreation Trail, this path is named for the abundant white trillium that grows along its route in spring. Climb along the edge of a deep ravine and follow the trail as it curves to the right, crossing the primary stream. The trail ascends higher along a tributary before turning southward.

Bypass the **Ravine Trail (RT)** and **Beech Trail (BT)**, winding atop the ridge on the **Moon Ridge Trail (MRT)**. Bear right on the **Twin Oaks Trail (TOT)**, descending toward the **Nature Center Building (NC)**. Angle left onto the **Lower**

*Scene along
the Meadow Trail*

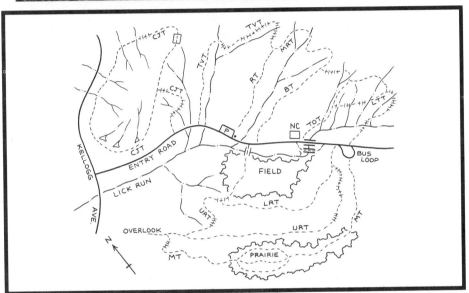

CALIFORNIA WOODS NATURE PRESERVE

Thicket Trail (LTT), crossing several small streams (see map); at the eastern end of the loop the route crosses Lick Run Creek and then ascends to the Preserve's roadway.

Turn right along the road and pick up the **Upper (URT) and Lower (LRT) Ridge Trails** just west of the bus loop. Ascend the stairs and bear left on the **Upper Ridge Trail (URT).** Hike westward along the crest of the ridge which yields broad views during the winter months. Bypass the Overlook and **Meadow Trail (MT)** cutoff, descending into the Lick Run valley via broad switchbacks. Cross the field to the bridge and turn left to reach your car.

Meadow Loop (1.5 miles). From the parking lot, walk eastward along the road- way, crossing Lick Run. Continue to the Bus Loop and pick up the **Meadow Trail (MT).** This path crosses through open woods and soon emerges at the edge of the Preserve's .5 acre, reconstructed prairie. Planted with tallgrass and wildflower species that characterized Ohio's pre-agricultural grasslands, the prairie harbors a vast array of plant and animal life.

After perusing the grassland, continue along the **Meadow Trail,** climbing onto the wooded ridge. Turn right at the trail intersection and then left on the **Upper Ridge Trail (URT),** descending into the Lick Run Valley. Cross the bridge and turn left on the roadway, returning to your car.

46 STANBERY PARK

Stanbery Creek Trail
Distance: 1.5 miles
Terrain: hilly; steep areas

Stanbery Park's 31 acres sprawl across the western flank of the Mt. Washington ridge, just east of the lower Little Miami Valley. The former estate of General Sanford Stanbery and his wife, Mamie, the land was acquired by the city of Cincinnati in 1940, and is managed by the Cincinnati Park Board.

The **Stanbery's old, stone house (1)** still stands on the property. Just east of the house is a **bronze statue/fountain (2)** depicting a young boy with a book. The statue, cast in Yellow Springs, Ohio was erected in 1938 by the Civic Club of Mt. Washington.

The Park's trails are somewhat rugged, with steep areas, narrow catwalks and slippery stream crossings.

Directions:

To reach Stanbery Park from downtown Cincinnati, follow Columbia Parkway (U.S. 50) east for approximately 4.5 miles. Turn right on Stanley Ave., drive 2 blocks and turn left on Kellogg Ave. (U.S. 52). Drive 2.3 miles and bear right onto Salem Pike, which circles back across Kellogg Ave. and winds up the Mt. Washington ridge. Follow this road for 2.1 miles and turn left on Sutton Rd. Drive 1.4 miles, curve to the right for 1 block and turn left on Oxford Ave. The Park entrance will be ½ block on your left.

Route:

The main route, known as the **Stanbery Creek Trail (A)**, is included in the Na-
tional Recreation Trail system. This 1.5 mile loop winds along the primary forks of Stanbery Creek, connected to the ridgetop path by spur trails (see map).

Enter the trail just west of the parking lot, adjacent to a **yellow post (3)**. Wind downstream through a beautiful ravine speckled with huge beech trees. Side loops lead down to the creek where small waterfalls splash over ledges of shale and limestone. Fossil hunters will find numerous bryozoans and brachiopods in these ancient, Ordovician rocks.

Just past the **primary streamside loop (4)**, the trail narrows and clings to the edge of the cliff, crossing two small bridges. It then descends to the creek bed, crosses the stream and follows the western bank for a short distance.

Recross the creek where another **trail (B)** climbs to the **ridgetop shelter (5)**. Continue downstream along the creek's eastern bank and follow the trail as it curves to the right and gently ascends along the north fork of Stanbery Creek. After crossing numerous side streams the trail emerges from the forest at the bottom of the Park's **Meadowland Natural Area (6)**. Climb this hillside and return to the lot, completing a 1.5 mile loop.

As is evident from the map, one can lengthen or shorten the hike by choosing alternative routes. The "B" trail, descending from the shelter to Stanbery Creek, is relatively gentle and footing is good. However, the "C" trail is precipitous and should be avoided by most hikers.

Waterfall on Stanbery Creek

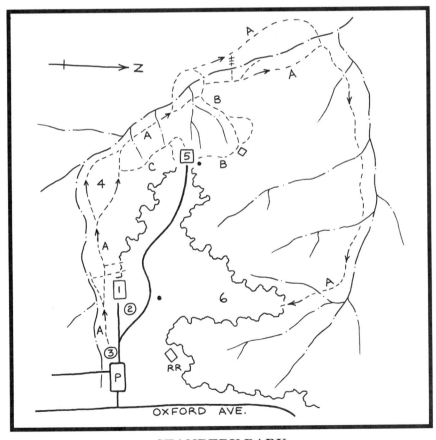

STANBERY PARK

47 WITHROW NATURE PRESERVE

Trout Lily Trail
   Distance: 2.0 miles
   Terrain:
      Old Farm Loop: rolling
      Hepatica Hill Loop: hilly, steep areas

Thanks to the generosity of Eugene and Adelaide Farny and through the efforts of the Ohio Nature Conservancy, Cincinnatians have a beautiful 273 acre refuge in eastern Hamilton County. **Withrow Nature Preserve**, added to the Park District in October, 1983, is well known for its great variety of wildflowers. Forest wildflowers peak in April and early May while grassland species adorn the meadows throughout warmer months.

Directions:

From I-275 in eastern Hamilton County, take Exit #69 (Five Mile Road). Head southwest on Five Mile Road, descending toward the Ohio River. The entry road to Withrow Nature Preserve will be approximately 1 mile ahead, on your left. A nominal day-use fee is charged or you may purchase an annual pass to all Hamilton County Parks.

Route:

The **Trout Lily Trail** is a double-loop route, combining the **Old Farm Loop** (**OFL; 1.75 miles**) and the **Hepatica Hill Loop** (**HHL; .25 mile**). A common entry trail begins just south of the parking area (*).

Walk a short distance, descend a stairway and bear left onto the **Old Farm Loop**. A winding route crosses two streams and skirts the upper reaches of smaller tributaries. Turn right at the trail inter-

section, curving through the woods to the edge of a large field.

Bear right once again, hiking through the forest to a fine overlook of the Ohio River Valley. Backtrack from the overlook and bear right on the **Old Farm Loop**, paralleling a drainage and eventually crossing the primary stream via a bridge. Curving eastward the trail passes an old cabin (C). Continue out to a transmission tower (T) where the primary trail angles to the left and soon enters an old farm field. Take the first cutoff on your left (see map) and follow this trail back to the entry path for the **Old Farm Loop**. White-tailed deer may be spotted on the meadows at dawn or dusk and great horned owls patrol the fields at night.

Wind back through the forest to the **Hepatica Hill Loop (HHL)** and turn left. Wildflowers are abundant along this trail in April and May. A brochure, published by the Park District, illustrates some of the plants that may be found here. These include trout lilies, hepatica, shooting star, trillium, Dutchman's breeches, squirrel corn, bloodroot, bluebells and Christmas ferns.

Snaking through the forest, the trail angles to the left and descends a stairway. It then turns northward and roller-coasters through the woodland before climbing the ridge via a series of stairs and decks. The **Hepatica Hill Loop** emerges from the forest behind the Highwood Lodge; turn left and walk back to the parking lot.

Crossing a meadow on the Old Farm Loop

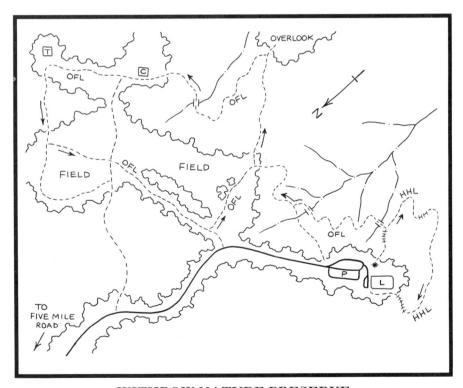

WITHROW NATURE PRESERVE

48 WOODLAND MOUND PARK

Combined Trail (Hedgeapple & Parcours)
   Distance: 1.8 miles
   Terrain: hilly; steep areas

Seasongood Nature Trail
   Distance: .75 mile
   Terrain: hilly; stairways

Cincinnati's numerous hills and ridges are heavily wooded. Extensive views are achieved only where roads or parks hug the edge of a cliff.

Woodland Mound Park, near the eastern border of Hamilton County, is an exception to that rule. Sprawling across a ridgetop, the Park's central corridor has been cleared of trees. Forest cloaks the hillsides but grasslands, ball fields and playgrounds give the area an unusual openness along the Ohio Valley.

A site for the Park was first targeted in the 1930s. After many years of land acquisition, Woodland Mound Park was finally dedicated in July, 1980. It now covers 900 acres and is a popular site for picnics, day hikes and nature study. A constant breeze atop this ridge makes for a cool retreat in summer and attracts kite flyers throughout the warmer months.

Seasongood Nature Center (NC) houses natural history exhibits, a small bookstore and Park offices. At the edge of the ridge, the **Weston Amphitheater (A)** seats 10,000 on its sloping lawn and is the site of various concerts throughout the summer months.

Directions:
From I-275 in eastern Hamilton County, take the Beechmont Avenue/Ohio Route 125 Exit (Exit #65) and head west on Beechmont Avenue. Drive .9 mile and turn left on Nordyke Road. Proceed 2 miles to the Park entrance, on your right. A nominal day-use fee is charged or you may purchase an annual pass to all Hamilton County Parks.

Routes:
There are several day hikes at Woodland Mound Park; we recommend the following routes.

Seasongood Nature Trail (.75 mile). Those interested in a short stroll through the woods should consider the **Seasongood Nature Trail (NT)** which begins at the **Nature Center (NC).**

After descending a hillside the trail crosses a creek via a wooden bridge, ascends a stairway and then forks. Take either path and complete a loop through this young, deciduous forest. The Park District offers a trail guide which lists many of the plants that inhabit the woodland.

After completing the loop, return to the Nature Center via your entry route.

The Seasongood Nature Center

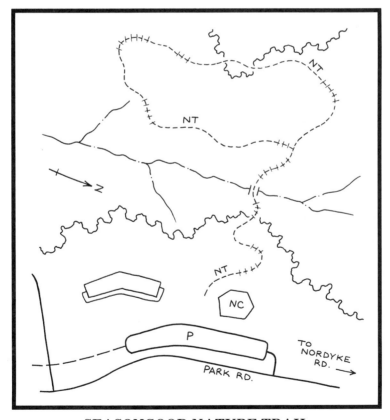

SEASONGOOD NATURE TRAIL

Combined Trail (1.8 miles). This day hike begins at the Weston Amphitheater parking lot and combines a walk to the Amphitheater with hikes along the **Hedgeapple (HT)** and **Parcours (PCT) Trails.** Head out to the Amphitheater which commands a spectacular view of the Ohio River Valley. Except for distant power plants, the view is remarkably free of modern structures.

Backtrack toward the parking lot and angle onto the **Hedgeapple Trail (HT).** Named for the hedgeapple (osage orange) trees that are common here, this .6 mile loop dips through the forest, taking a figure-eight route (see map). The trail is steep and footing is uneven in some areas. Near the bottom of the loop, a frog pond provides entertainment for children and a reststop for adults during the warmer months.

After completing the Hedgeapple Trail, turn right and pick up the Park's one-mile **Parcours Trail (PCT).** Follow this wide path as it skirts a meadow and then descends into a shallow ravine. Bear right at the trail intersection, cross the creek and ascend a short stairway. Turn right, paralleling the stream along a level, hillside path. Follow the trail as it curves to the left and circles a clearing where stone steps, a rock wall and other artifacts attest to the history of an abandoned homestead of this site. After a respite at this peaceful spot, retrace your route to the parking lot.

Woodland Mound's Parcours Trail

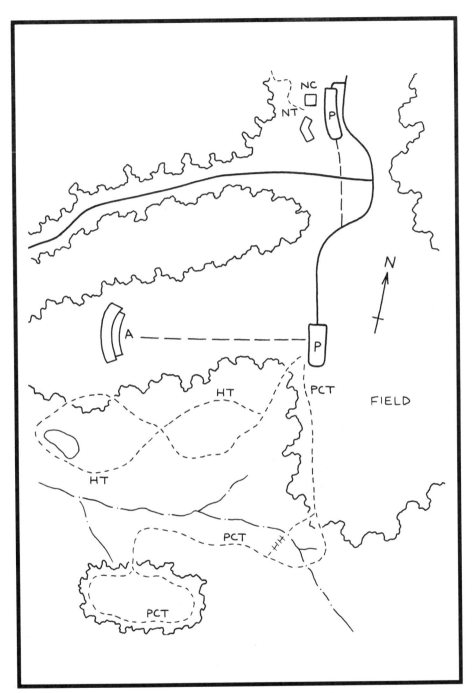

WOODLAND MOUND PARK

49 BOONE COUNTY CLIFFS STATE NATURE PRESERVE

Main Trail Loop
Distance: 2.0 miles
Terrain: hilly

East Boundary Loop
Distance: 1.0 mile
Terrain: hilly

The Kansan Glacier, the second major advance during the Pleistocene "Ice Age," plowed deep into western Ohio and eastern Indiana 1.2 million years ago. This massive ice sheet blocked the course of the Teays River which headed in the Virginia Appalachians and flowed northwestward through what is now Ohio, Indiana and Illinois. Diverted to the south and fueled by meltwater from the Kansan Glacier, the Teays gave rise to the Ohio River system which spilled to the southwest.

Outwash from the Kansan Glacier spread sand, gravel and other "till sediments" across northern Kentucky and southern Indiana which have since hardened into sheets of "conglomerate" rock. Subsequest erosion along the Ohio Valley has exposed outcrops of this conglomerate which, being more resistent than overlying sediments, forms impressive cliffs along stream channels.

One of the best places to see these conglomerate cliffs is at the **Boone County Cliffs State Nature Preserve,** east of Burlington. This 75-acre refuge, cloaked with old growth forest and dissected by spring-fed streams, was brought under the protection of the Kentucky State Nature Preserve Commission through the efforts of the Kentucky Chapter of the Nature Conservancy. Access to the Preserve is provided by two trail loops, described below.

Directions:

From I-75 in northern Kentucky, take the Florence/Burlington Exit (Exit #181) and head west on Kentucky Route 18. Drive 10.3 miles and turn left on a small road that crosses a bridge where a sign indicates "Kentucky Nature Conservancy

1.9 miles." This turnoff is approximately 6 miles east of Burlington.

Follow the small road for almost 2 miles to a graveled lot on your left. A sign and visitor registration box indicate that you have reached the Boone County Cliffs State Nature Preserve. The Preserve is open dawn to dusk.

Routes:

The Nature Preserve is accessed by two trail loops.

Main Trail Loop (2.0 miles). The **Main Trail (MT)** begins next to the visitor registration box, makes a curve to the west and then climbs along the east wall of the Preserve's central gorge via stairways and a winding route. After negotiating the first outcropping of Kansan conglomerate, the **Main Trail** winds eastward above a tributary where the **East Boundary Trail (EBT)** cuts off to the right (see map).

Continue along the **Main Trail** which begins a long excursion across the upper reaches of the central gorge, crossing numerous drainages along the way. Curving back to the southwest, the trail runs atop a narrow ridge where deep ravines cut away to either side. After a sharp bend to the east, watch for an intersection with the **Ridge Loop Trail (RLT)**. Bear left onto this short loop which takes you out to the edge of the conglomerate cliffs; this rocky overlook offers a broad view across the central gorge of the Preserve and is a fine spot for a picnic lunch (be sure to pack out your leftovers and trash).

Continue along the **Ridge Loop Trail,** rejoining the **Main Trail** which leads southward across the forested ridge. Curving to the east, the trail descends to the creek and follows it downstream for a

Cliffs of Kansan conglomerate line the central gorge.

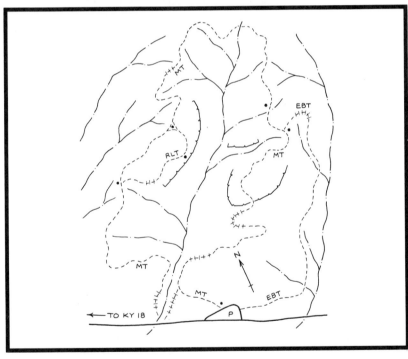

BOONE COUNTY CLIFFS

short distance. Just before reaching the roadway, the trail crosses the creek. Return to the parking lot by walking along the road or by taking the spur trail which ascends along the creek (see map).

East Boundary Loop (1.0 mile). The **East Boundary Trail (EBT)** leaves the east end of the parking lot, parallels the roadway and then angles to the north, ascending through a valley. After crossing a major tributary, the trail climbs along this stream and curves above its upper reaches on a long stairway.

Upon intersecting the **Main Trail (MT)**, bear left and descend to the parking area along its eastern arm (see map). Along the way you will cross an outcropping of the Kansan conglomerate, a fine spot for a reststop and picnic lunch.

121

50 DOE RUN LAKE

North Shore Trail
  Distance: 2.2 miles roundtrip
  Terrain: rolling

Loop Trail
  Distance: .5 mile
  Terrain: hilly

Sometimes the best hikes are found at the least known places. Such is the case at **Doe Run Lake,** a hidden jewel in Kenton County. Used primarily by local fishermen, the lake and surrounding forest offer a peaceful retreat near the rapidly developing suburbs of Northern Kentucky.

Directions:
  From the southern portion of I-275, east of I-75, take the Covington/Independence Exit (Exit #80) and head south on Kentucky Route 17 (Madison Pike). Drive 2.5 miles and turn right to "Old Kentucky 17;" this is the second turnoff to Old 17 when coming south from I-275.
  After turning off New Kentucky 17, cross the creek and bear left onto Bullock Pen Road (marked by a Doe Run Lake sign); this road cuts under a railroad trestle and leads to Doe Run Lake. Park in the lot at the south end of the dam.

Routes:
  The **North Shore Trail (NST; our terminology)** begins at the north end of the dam where a path from the parking lot meets a short trail that descends from the entry road (see map). This wide, graveled path leads westward above the north shore of Doe Run Lake, crossing stream beds along the way. Views of the Lake, more expansive in winter, are spaced along the route.
  After hiking approximately 1 mile you will reach a clearing near the Bullock Pen

Creek inlet, where numerous side trails lead down to the lake and creek. The main trail continues upstream, cutting across a sunny meadow and soon descends to **Bullock Pen Creek.** This is an excellent destination for a picnic lunch; a low waterfall, just downstream from the crossing, adds to the serenity and children will enjoy wading in the shallows. Fossil hunters will find plenty of bryozoans and brachiopods in the Ordovician rocks that line the stream.
  Those who return to the parking area from this creekside retreat will achieve a day hike of 2.2 miles. If you're up for additional exercise, throw in the **Loop Trail (LT),** a half-mile excursion across the wooded ridge south of Bullock Pen Creek. Cross the stream, angle to the right and then bear left on a trail that climbs steeply through the forest (see map). Leveling out atop the ridge, this trail eventually leads to a field; though the path enters the field, this is private land we recommend backtracking to the **Loop Trail** (see map).
  The western portion of the **Loop Trail** descends very steeply to Bullock Pen Creek where it intersects a creekside path. Turn right and follow this trail back to the **North Shore Trail (NST).** Along the way you will cross and re-cross the creek; bypass a cutoff on your left, just before the second stream crossing (see map). Return to the parking area along the **North Shore Trail,** completing a total hike of 2.7 miles.

The North Shore Trail

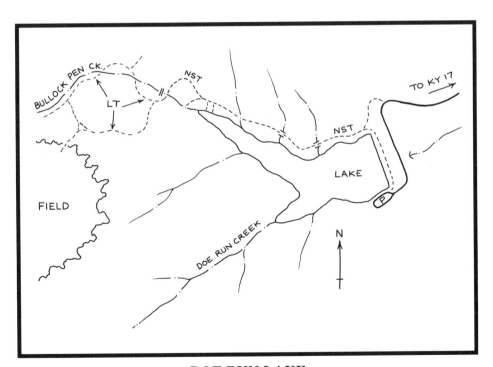

DOE RUN LAKE

51 HIGHLAND CEMETERY FOREST PRESERVE

Trail #1
Distance: 1.25 miles
Terrain: hilly

Trail #2
Distance: .5 mile
Terrain: hilly

Trail #3
Distance: .75 mile
Terrain: hilly

Enamored with the natural beauty of **Highland Cemetery**, Gayle Pille approached the Superintendent with her idea of placing bluebird boxes on the Cemetery's open meadows. To her delight the Cemetery Board was receptive to her project and informed her of their plans to enhance wildlife habitat throughout the Cemetery as a gift to the local community. Indeed, Gayle was enlisted to create a trail system for Highland Cemetery's forest preserve.

A member of the Kenton County Conservation Board and the Kentucky Trail Advisory Committee, Ms. Pille organized a group of volunteers who designed and constructed the current trail network from 1990 through 1991. The trails meander through a rich, hardwood forest that cloaks the eastern edge of the Cemetery. Wildflower gardens and wildlife food plots have also been developed on the grounds.

Highland Cemetery, the second largest cemetery in Kentucky, was formally dedicated on June 22, 1869. Covering 300 acres and having registered over 40,000 burials, the Cemetery occupies the site of a Civil War ammunitions depot. Thirteen Civil War soldiers, including Confederate General James Morrison Hawes, are buried at the Cemetery and trail construction volunteers unearthed a Civil War cannonball in the forest preserve.

Directions:

From I-75 in northern Kentucky, take Exit #188-A. Highland Cemetery is just southeast of the Interstate on the east side of Dixie Highway (U.S. 127). Enter the main gate, pass the Cemetery office and continue to bear right at the intersections, eventually passing a lake. Park along the Cemetery drive near Lucerne Avenue (see map).

Route:

Three trails provide access to Highland Cemetery's forest preserve. We suggest the following **combined route** which yields a hike of approximately 2.75 miles.

Pick up **Trail #1** at the forest edge and descend into the woods along the Cemetery boundary. **Trail #1**, blazed with orange paint, soon angles to the left and rollercoasters along the west wall of a deep ravine. Crossing numerous tributaries the route eventually forks; bear right onto **Trail #2**, blazed with red paint, which descends toward the creek. Near the bottom of the slope, the remnants of an old well (W) sit along the trail.

As is too often the case in urban areas, new "development" is encroaching on this forest preserve. Just across the valley, a modern, 4-lane highway (Highland Avenue) has cut a swath through the long undisturbed woods. **Trail #2** curves to the northwest, climbing above a major tributary and soon intersects **Trail #1**. Bear right (straight ahead) on **Trail #1**, cross under a power line and begin a slow descent to a stream crossing.

On the opposite side of the creek is the cutoff to **Trail #3**. Turn right and follow this trail which is blazed with blue paint. After crossing a drainage the trail forks.

*The trails
provide access
to a rich
deciduous forest*

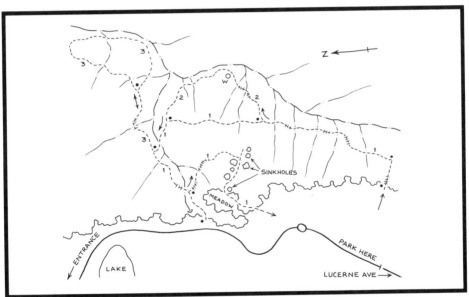

HIGHLAND CEMETERY FOREST PRESERVE

Take either route and complete a .4 mile loop through the forest, passing near the main creek at your lowest point.

After completing the **Trail #3 loop,** continue upstream along **Trail #1.** Just after crossing the main tributary the route forks; the right fork continues along the stream and climbs directly to the Cemetery Road. Take the left fork which ascends a stairway, dips through another ravine and then climbs to an area with numerous sinkholes. Turn right at the intersection passing more sinkholes and a woodland meadow on your way to the Cemetery Road. Return to your car by hiking along the road.

52 DEVOU PARK

Nature Trail
 Distance: 1.25 miles
 Terrain: hilly; steep areas

Overlook Hike
 Distance 2.2 miles
 Terrain: rolling

To many Cincinnatians, **Devou Park** in Northern Kentucky, is known for two things. First, it harbors a spectacular view of Covington and the Cincinnati basin. Second, it's hard to find.

Devou Park's 550 ridgetop acres were donated to the city of Covington in 1910. For an overview of the Park, we suggest the following two hikes.

Directions:

Follow I-75 south into Kentucky and take the Ky. 1072/Ft. Wright Exit (Exit #189-B). Bear right off the exit and turn right onto Dixie Highway. Drive 1 block and turn left on Sleepy Hollow Rd. (Ky. 1072). Bear left and wind downhill. Drive 1.7 miles to the Park's entrance, on your right (just before the railroad trestle).

Follow Devou Park Rd. until it deadends into Montague (see map). Turn right and then bear right into the golf course/tennis area. Park in the lot adjacent to the **clubhouse (1)**.

Routes:

Nature Trail. Devou Park's 1.25 mile Nature Trail originates along the gravel service road that crosses between the **golf course (2)** and the **tennis complex (3)**. Hike westward along the road until it turns sharply to the left. Find the trail to the right of this bend (see map) and descend into the ravine via a series of switchbacks and stairways.

Near the bottom, the trail loops to the left, following a small creek, and then turns upstream along the primary channel. Angling to the left, ascend the hillside,

crossing the service road, and wind through the ridgetop forest. Turn left at the trail intersection, as illustrated on the map. The trail eventually emerges from the woodland near the tennis courts.

The Sierra Club of Northern Kentucky has directed efforts to improve Devou Park's Nature Trail.

Overlook Hike. Unfortunately, except for the Nature Trail, Devou Park does not currently provide hike/bike paths for exercise conscious visitors. The following walk to **Lookout Point (4)**, from the **clubhouse area, (1)**, thus parallels the Park's roadways, crossing open lawns along the way.

Walk northward on Montague and turn right at the first intersection (see map), passing the Park's **natural amphitheater (5)**. Bear right and wind downhill along West Park Rd. Turn left at the intersection, climbing the ridge, and bear right into the Lookout area. From the overlook the visitor enjoys an expansive view of Covington, the Ohio Valley and the Cincinnati basin, flanked by ridgetop neighborhoods.

Return along Park Lane which merges with Jerol Ave. Be sure to stop at the **Behringer-Crawford Museum (6)** which houses a collection of artifacts, maps and exhibits, depicting the natural history and early industries of Northern Kentucky. The Museum is open Tuesday through Saturday, 10 am to 5 pm and Sunday, 1 pm to 5 pm. It is closed on Mondays, most holidays and during the month of January. A small admission fee is charged.

Follow Montague Rd. back to the clubhouse area, completing a loop of 2.2 miles.

The Cincinnati basin from Devou Park

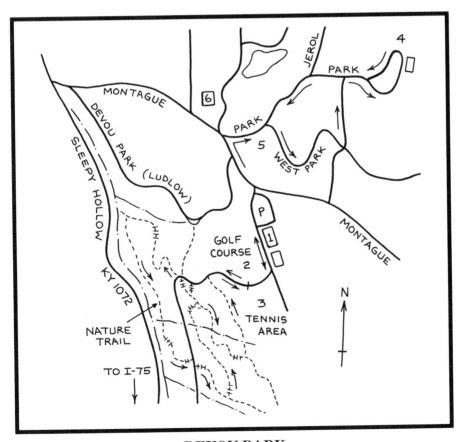

DEVOU PARK

53 WEST COVINGTON/MAINSTRASSE

Distance: 2.7 miles
Terrain: flat

The original settlement of **Covington,** Kentucky, nestled in the west Licking Valley, was platted in 1815. The town was bounded by 6th and Washington Sts. and by the Ohio and Licking Rivers. Incorporated as a city in 1835, Covington expanded to the south and west.

The **West Side District** was the second major addition to the city's original layout. Bordered to the west by Willow Run Creek, this neighborhood was sparsely settled until the influx of German immigrants in the 1840's. Much of the District's land had been owned by James Riddle, who operated a farm, mill, distillery and ferry service from his west Covington property. When the Bank of the United States foreclosed on Riddle's estate in 1830, the land was opened for residential settlement.

The German immigrants built closely spaced "rowhouses" which still typify the area today. In an effort to preserve these structures and to draw tourists to this historic district, the MainStrasse Village Association was formed in 1978. With the aid of a $2.5 million grant from Kentucky's Board of Tourism, many homes and commercial buildings have been restored. The core of this redevelopment is centered around the intersection of 6th and Main Streets, where shops have clustered along the open mall. Covington's West Side District was added to the National Register of Historic Places in 1982.

Directions:

To reach **MainStrasse Village** from Cincinnati, cross the Suspension Bridge and follow Court Ave. to 4th St. Turn right (west), drive 6½ blocks and turn left on Philadelphia St., which borders Goebel Park (see map). Alternatively, follow I-75 to the Covington/Ludlow Exit (Exit #192),

turn east on 5th St. and turn right on Philadelphia.

For a walking tour of the District, park along Philadelphia St. which borders **Goebel Park (1).**

Route:

The Park's **clock tower (2),** constructed in the late 1970's reflects the German heritage of the neighborhood. Walk east along 6th St. The dome and steeples of the **Mother of God Church (4)** loom in the distance. The 6th St. Mall, site of Covington's annual Oktoberfest, is lined with shops that retain the flavor of the mid 1800's. A **fountain (3),** depicting a girl carrying two geese, graces the corner of 6th and main.

Continue east on 6th St., pass under the railroad bridge, bearing right and then left. The **Mother of God Church (4),** at 6th and Washington was built in 1871. Organized in 1841 by Rev. Ferdinand Kuhr, this is the second oldest parish in Covington. The Church's dome was destroyed by fire on September 25, 1986, but was rebuilt within a year. Its twin steeples rise 200 ft. above the city and the building's interior is adorned with stained glass, frescoes and murals of German origin. Across 6th St. from the Church, **Tickets, (5),** a restaurant and nightclub, occupies an old firehouse, dating from the mid 1800's.

Continue east for 1 block and turn right (south) along Madison Ave., Covington's true "Main St." Walk ½ block and turn right on Pike St., lined with shops. This leads into 7th Street (see map). Continue west for 1 block and turn left along Russell St.

Russell St. is lined with refurbished, closely-spaced homes which typify this historic area. The **Sandford House (7),** in the 1000 block, dates from the early 1800's. Built on land originally owned by General Thomas Sandford, Northern Kentucky's first Congressman, the house was purchased

128

*Fountain on
the 6th St. Mall*

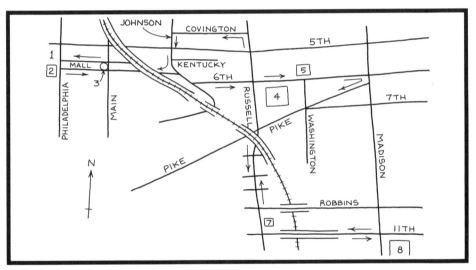

WEST COVINGTON/MAINSTRASSE

by the Western Baptist Theologic Institute in 1835. The Institute closed in 1853 due to dissension over the slavery issue.

Turn left (east) on 11th St., cross the bridge and descend to Madison Ave. The **Cathedral Basilica of the Assumption (8)**, dedicated in 1901, fills most of the block to the southeast. Its facade is modeled after the Notre Dame Cathedral, in Paris. Three frescoes by Frank Duveneck, Covington's native son and a former Dean at Cincinnati's Art Academy, adorn the Church's interior.

Retrace your route along 11th and Russell Sts. Continue north on Russell, crossing over 6th and 5th Sts. Turn left along Covington Ave., a cobblestone alley lined with attractive, 19th Century rowhouses.

Turn left (south) on Johnson St. Kentucky Ave., on your left between 5th and 6th Sts., is another block of fine, refurbished rowhouses. Turn right on 6th St. and return to Goebel Park. Your walking tour of West Covington/MainStrasse has totalled 2.7 miles.

54 COVINGTON RIVERSIDE DISTRICT AND SUSPENSION BRIDGE

Distance: 2.5 miles
Terrain: mostly flat; few stairways

A walk through **Covington's Riverside Drive Historic District** is easily combined with a stroll across Greater Cincinnati's most famous bridge.

Directions:
Park in one of the lots along Pete Rose Way, just west of **Riverfront Stadium (1)**.

Route:
Cross the road and ascend the stairs to the bridge's entry ramp (see map).

The **John A. Roebling Suspension Bridge (2)** opened to traffic on New Year's Day, 1867, after ten years of construction. Its architect, John Roebling, used this experience in his later design of New York's Brooklyn Bridge. The Suspension Bridge stretches 2252 feet across the Ohio and is the oldest bridge that still spans the River today.

Just southwest of the bridge is **Covington Landing (3)**, a hotel-restaurant-entertainment complex that opened in 1990.

At the south end of the bridge, turn left along E. 2nd St. for ½ block and then left on Greenup St. The **Riverside Plaza Condominiums (4)**, at E. 2nd and Greenup, are part of Covington's Riverside Development Project. The complex consists of two buildings, Riverside Terrace, completed in 1984, and Riverside Plaza, which opened in 1986. Combined, the buildings contain 85 units, including modern townhouses designed to blend with the nearby **Shinkle Row (16)**. Many of the units open onto terraced decks, overlooking the Ohio River.

North of the Condominium complex is a bronze **statue of John A. Roebling (5)**, architect of the Suspension Bridge. It is one of seven statues that are spaced along Covington's Riverside Walk, depicting individuals who played important roles in the city's development. The bronze statues

were dedicated in October, 1988.

Walk east along Riverside Drive which is lined with large, ante-bellum houses. Strolling down this majestic avenue, one is reminded of southern port cities such as Charleston and Savannah. On the southeast corner of Garrard St. and Riverside Drive is **George Rogers Clark Park**, adorned with **statues of Simon Kenton (6)** and **Captain Mary B. Greene (7)**. Simon Kenton, one of the first men to explore and settle the Covington area, is the person for whom Kenton County was named. Captain Greene was one of the few women to command a riverboat, playing an important role in the city's early economy.

Further east along Riverside Drive, **James Bradley (8)** relaxes on a bench. An eloquent abolitionist and former slave, Mr. Bradley took part in the famous Lane Seminary Debates.

At the junction of Riverside Drive and Shelby St. are two more figures. **Chief Little Turtle (9)**, leader of the Miami Indian tribe, points across the Ohio while **John James Audubon (10)**, the renowned naturalist and artist, faces the mouth of the Licking River.

Angle south along Shelby St., passing a cluster of new townhomes. Turn right on E. 2nd St. The **Mimosa House Museum (11)**, built in 1853, is an original Italianate structure that underwent Colonial-Revival restoration in 1900. Daniel Fallis, a prominent Cincinnati banker, and his descendents occupied the house from 1861 to 1950. Today, the building is operated as a house museum by a nonprofit organization. Tours of the house are conducted on weekends, from 1 to 6 pm; a fee is charged.

The **Lowry-Laidley House (12)**, at 404 E. 2nd St., was constructed about 1870. It offers an example of Italiante architecture, complete with mansard roof and Victorian Gothic moldings.

130

Scene along Covington's Riverside Walk

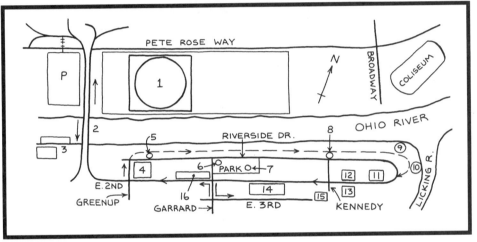

COVINGTON RIVERSIDE DISTRICT

The **Carneal House (13)**, more properly called the Gano-Southgate House, sits above the southeast corner of Kennedy and E. 2nd St. Built in 1815, it is the oldest brick house in Covington and is thought to have been built for John S. Gano, the city's founder. A tunnel, used to hide runaway slaves, leads from its basement to the west bank of the Licking River.

Continuing west on E. 2nd St. you will pass the **Governors Point Condominiums (14)** which occupy the former site and structure of Wm. Booth Memorial Hospital. The central, 5-story building dates from the mid 1920s.

Turn left (south) on Garrard St. and then left on E. 3rd St. The **former home of Daniel Carter Beard (15)**, first National Commissioner of the Boy Scouts of America,

sits at the east end of the block. This 1820 Victorian home has been designated a National Historic Landmark. Beard, whose statue graces the home, founded the "Sons of Daniel Boone" which became the Boy Scouts of America in 1910.

Backtrack along Third and Garrard Streets and turn left along E. 2nd. The **Shinkle Row Houses (16)** were officially recognized by the Miami Purchase Association in 1976, honoring their attractive and detailed restoration.

Continue west on E. 2nd St. and then re-cross the Suspension Bridge. Your scenic and historic tour has totalled 2.5 miles. For more information on this interesting area, contact the Licking Riverside Civic Association.

Distance: 2.5 miles
Terrain: flat

Founded by General James Taylor and his wife, Keturah Moss Leach, in 1795, **Newport** played a vital role in the development of Northern Kentucky. General Taylor, a cousin of President Zachary Taylor, had inherited 1500 acres along the Ohio River from his father and decided to use the land as a nidus for his pioneer settlement. The Taylors, natives of Virginia, named the city after Captain Christopher Newport, the English naval officer who commanded the first voyage to Jamestown.

Newport's development was assured with the establishment of a U.S. military outpost, **Newport Barracks**, at the confluence of the Licking and Ohio Rivers in 1804. By the end of the 19th Century, the city had become a thriving residential and business community, tied to Cincinnati by a "modern" streetcar line.

A 2.5 mile walk, described below, takes you past some of Newport's most historic buildings and homes.

Directions:

From downtown Cincinnati, take the L&N bridge across the Ohio River and continue south on Saratoga. Proceed to 4th St. and turn right (west). Drive 3 blocks and turn right on Columbia; at the end of the street, pass through the levee and turn left. Proceed to **General James Taylor Park (1)**.

Route:

Leave your car at **General James Taylor Park (1)**, the former site of the **Newport Barracks**. Established in 1804, this military outpost served as a prison during the War of 1812 and as headquarters for the South District of the U.S. Army until the Civil War. The military post moved to Fort Thomas in 1893 and its land was donated to the city of Newport the following

year. As is evident from the introduction, the Park is named for the founding father of Newport.

Walk eastward past **"Riverboat Row (2)"** where a string of barges have been converted to restaurants and nightclubs, each enjoying a fabulous view of downtown Cincinnati. Pass through the levee and walk up Columbia to Third St.; turn left on Third and follow this street for six blocks (see map).

St. Paul's Episcopal Church (3) was founded in 1844; the present-day stone church graced with fine stained-glass windows, was built in 1871. The **Richard Southgate Home (4)**, at 24 East Third St., was the birthplace of General John Thompson, inventor of semi-automatic rifles and inspirational father of the submachine gun. **Otto Zimmerman & Son Company (5)**, at Third and Saratoga, was founded in Cincinnati in 1876. The Company moved to its Newport plant in 1921 where it is still operated by members of the Zimmerman family.

Cross Washington, entering the Mansion Hill Historic District. The **Taylor Mansion (6)**, christened "Bellevue" by the Taylor family, commands a broad view of the Ohio River and sits at the center of the founding family's 1500 acre estate. This Greek Revival structure was built in 1840 and underwent extensive renovation in 1890.

Turn right on Overton. The Queen Anne style house at **301 Overton (7)** dates from 1889 while the Italianate townhouse at **311 Overton (8)**, furnished with a "Newport-Plan" porch, was completed in 1870. Turn left on 4th St. and then make a loop using Park Avenue, Lexington, Providence Way and 4th Street (see map). The **500 block of 4th Street (9)**, known as "Queen Anne

Campbell County Courthouse

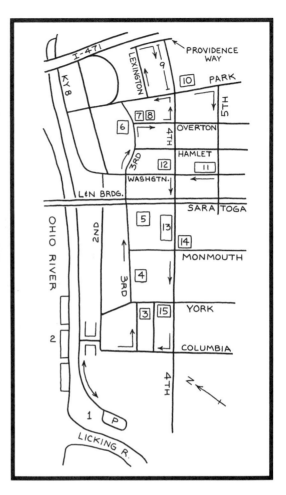

NEWPORT: CIVIC & MANSION HILL DISTRICT

Row," was home to many of Newport's most wealthy citizens during the late 1800s. The Colonial Revival house at **401 Park (10)**, now home to the Northern Kentucky District Health Department, was built by George Wiedemann Jr., son of the famous brewer, in 1899.

Turn left on Park, right on 5th and then right on Washington. The "row houses" at **413-421 Washington (11)** date from the late 1880s; their "shared-wall" construction style conserved space and materials, a common practice during that era. The **Saunders Mansion (12)**, at 4th & Washington, was built for a grand daughter of General James Taylor; this Italianate house, circa 1872, is now being converted to condominiums.

Head westward along 4th St. The **Fourth Street Elementary School (13)** opened in 1936; it occupies the former site of the **Newport Academy**, established in 1799, the second educational institution west of the Appalachians. Organized in 1898, the Newport Public Library (now the Campbell County Public Library) moved to **Carnegie Hall (14)** in 1902.

Further west is the **Campbell County Courthouse (15)**, designed by A.C. Nash and completed in 1884. Entered on the National Register of Historic Places in 1988, this magnificent building with its four-sided clock tower and mixed architectural style, stands on the site of the original log courthouse (circa 1799).

Turn right on Columbia and return to General James Taylor Park.

Distance: 1.6 miles
Terrain: flat

While the city was founded in 1795, the zenith of Newport's cultural, commercial and architectural history would not occur for almost a century. It was during the 1870s and 1880s that wealthy merchants and professionals flocked to the neighborhoods of eastern Newport, enticed by tree-lined streets and superbly crafted homes. Even today the mansions, houses and townhomes of east Newport reflect the quality, old-world craftmanship of the late 19th Century. Fine examples of Victorian, Queen Anne, Italianate and Colonial Revival architecture are found throughout the community.

Though many of these homes bear the scars of hard economic times, urban renewal has flourished in Newport and the effort to protect and renovate these architectural gems is readily apparent to any visitor. As a tribute to this spirit of preservation, we offer a 1.6 mile walking tour of **Newport's East Row Historic District**; all buildings within the District have been listed on the National Register of Historic Places.

Directions:

From downtown Cincinnati, take the L&N bridge across the Ohio River. Turn left on 3rd Street, proceed 1 block and turn right on Washington. Park in the lot on the east side of Washington, between 5th and 6th Streets (see map).

Route:

Walk to the corner of 6th and Washington. **Pompillio's Restaurant (1)**, at 600 Washington, has long been a favorite of Italian food lovers; the restaurant gained additional fame as the locale for a scene in the movie "Rainman." **Watertower Square (2)**, now a collection of factory outlet shops, was the home of the Dueber Watch Case Factory in

the late 1800s.

Proceed east on 6th Street. The Italianate townhouse at **326 East 6th (3)** has been restored for use as a Bed & Breakfast. Further along, the **Central Christian Church (4)**, now the Bibleview Baptist Church, dates from 1895; its brick and stone facade is graced by stained-glass windows and a fine slate roof.

Turn left on Monroe and right on 5th Street, passing the **Trinity Baptist Church (5)**. Jog right on Park Avenue and continue eastward along Nelson Place. The Swiss Chalet home at **608 Nelson Place (6)**, circa 1899, was built by Judge John T. Hodge; Judge Hodge paid $8000 for the modest lot, a tidy sum in 1898. The house at **610 Nelson Place (7)**, built in 1903, offers a fine example of Colonial Revival architecture. Next door are the **Flora Apartments (8)**, circa 1915.

Turn right on Linden Avenue. The **Hannaford Apartments (9)**, designed by Cincinnati's famous architect, Samuel Hannaford, was completed in 1902; this Beaux-Arts building, originally Our Lady of Providence Academy, a Catholic girls' school, was converted to luxury apartments in 1985. Further south, at **619 Linden Avenue (10)**, is an excellent example of Foursquare style architecture, common in the early 1900s.

Turn right on 7th Street and then right on Maple. The houses at **610 and 626 Maple (11)** reflect the Colonial Revival style, popular throughout Newport at the turn of the Century. Proceed west along 6th Street and turn left on Monroe. A group of **Italianate townhomes (12)**, built in the early 1880s, will be on your left (603-611 Monroe). The house at **624 Monroe (13)** was first owned by B.H. and Mary Kroger, founders of the Kroger grocery

These attractive homes typify the East Row District

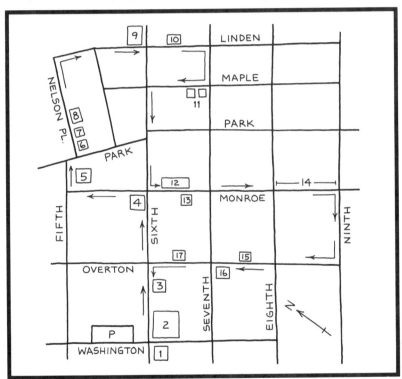

EAST ROW HISTORIC DISTRICT

chain. Most of the homes in the next two blocks date from the 1870s and 1880s, including a fine collection of "Newport Narrows" in the **800 block (14).**

Turn right on 9th and then right on Overton. The attractive home at **723 Overton (15)** dates from 1882 while the corner house at **702 Overton (16)** was built in 1878. The **First Presbyterian Church (17),** now the Christ Community Church, has graced this street since 1896.

Head west along 6th Street and return to your car.

57 BELLEVUE/DAYTON LEVEE WALK

Distance: 3.0 miles
Terrain: flat; some stairs

Originally part of General James Taylor's estate (see Walk #55), **Bellevue** was founded in 1866 by the General's great grandson and Campbell County congressman, Albert S. Berry. Since Bellevue was constructed well above the Ohio River, it was less prone to seasonal flooding than were other northern Kentucky cities, making it an attractive location for Cincinnati businessmen and professionals. By the turn of the Century, Bellevue was also renowned for its riverside bathing beaches, including "Queen City Beach," which enticed tourists from the eastern States. Channelization of the Ohio and increasing water pollution led to the demise of these resorts by the 1930s. To commemorate those glory days, the city of Bellevue plans to establish a park along its riverfront; the park will include a replica of a 1910 Bathhouse.

A 1.5 mile walk (3 miles roundtrip) takes you from the heart of Bellevue's **Fairfield Avenue Historic District,** along the Ohio River levee and out to the **Watertown Yacht Club,** which opened in 1989.

Directions:

From Cincinnati, follow I-471 south across the Ohio River and take the first exit in Kentucky. Proceed down to Kentucky Route 8 and head east. Drive approximately .8 mile into Bellevue, parking along Route 8 (Fairfield Ave.) in the city's business district.

Route:

Route 8 itself is often called the **Mary Ingles Highway,** honoring the first white woman to set foot in Kentucky. Mary was abducted by Shawnee Indians in her native Virginia, in 1755, and was brought to Kentucky. She escaped from her captors a year later, following the River back to the Virginia mountains.

In Bellevue, Route 8 is **Fairfield Avenue,** the central business corridor since the city's incorporation in 1870. Most of the buildings that line this avenue, especially those between the cross-streets of Taylor and O'Fallon, were constructed in the late 1800s or early 1900s and are now protected within the **Fairfield Avenue Historic District,** established in 1989. "Two-part Commercial Block" is the predominant architectural style, with retail or office space on the first floor and living quarters above. The **Marianne Theater,** at 609 Fairfield, dates from the 1930s; with its neon marquee and polychrome tile facade, it is considered to be one of the best preserved Art Deco theaters in Greater Cincinnati.

Walk eastward through the business district and turn left on O'Fallon Avenue. Proceed one block and climb onto the **Ohio River levee.** Within ¼ mile the levee curves to the northeast, paralleling the River and following the contour of **Dayton, Kentucky.** The Eden Park Water Tower (see Walk #40) is clearly visible across the River and views of Mt. Adams (Walk #41) soon unfold to the west. One-half mile along the levee you will pass the port of **Queen City Riverboats (QCR),** one of several companies that offer excursions along the Ohio River.

Another mile brings you to the **Watertown Yacht Club (WYC).** Completed in 1989, this man-made harbor provides safe mooring for over 500 boats. An indoor restaurant is open all year but the marina's outdoor bar and grille is especially inviting during the warmer months.

After rest and refreshment at the Yacht Club, return to your car via the same route, completing a roundtrip walk of 3 miles.

The Watertown Yacht Club

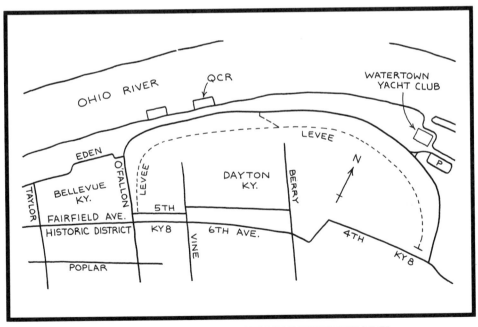

THE BELLEVUE/DAYTON LEVEE WALK

58 FORT THOMAS MILITARY RESERVATION/TOWER PARK

Distance: 1.4 miles
Terrain: flat

Ft. Thomas, Kentucky, sits 300 feet above the Ohio River Valley. Incorporated in 1914, the city formed around a Federal military outpost that was established on this high ridge in 1887. The Fort itself, replacing the floodprone Newport Barracks, was named for General George Thomas who fought in the Civil, Mexican and Indian Wars.

The city of Ft. Thomas acquired much of the Reservation in December, 1972, and established "**Tower Park**" on the site. The latter now includes playgrounds, tennis courts, a baseball field, a natural amphitheater and indoor athletic facilities at the refurbished Armory. The Federal Government still retains some residential structures and the Veterans Administration Nursing Home on the Reservation grounds.

A walk through this 111 acre preserve offers a pleasing blend of history and natural scenery.

Directions:

From I-471, take the Grand Ave./Ky. 1892 Exit (Exit #3). Turn east and follow Grand Ave. as it winds up the ridge. Drive 1.7 miles and turn right on S. Ft. Thomas Ave. Proceed 2 blocks to the Park entrance, on your left.

Park in one of the lots at the Douglas St. entrance (see map).

Route:

A 90-foot, limestone **tower**, constructed in 1898, stands near the entrance and commemorates soldiers of the 6th Regiment of the U.S. Infantry who fought in the Spanish American War.

Walk east along Cochran, past the Park's amphitheater (see map). This drive leads out to **Alexander Circle** where a cluster of brick homes enjoy a spectacular view of the Ohio River Valley. The view extends from Lunken Airport to the north and follows the River south, past Old Coney, Riverbend and River Downs. The Cincinnati Waterworks can be seen across from the Fort and the I-275 bridge spans the Ohio just south of the overlook. The houses on the Circle belong to the U.S. Government and are used by employees of the V.A. Nursing Home.

Return along the drive that passes to the north of the ball field (see map). Turn left and follow Cochran Ave. south. Green St., on your right, is lined with the former homes of military personnel, now occupied by Ft. Thomas residents. Continue along Cochran, passing the **Veterans Administration Nursing Home**. This building, completed in 1934, was initially used as a military barrack. It served briefly as an Air Force hospital in the 1950's before it became the Tristate region's V.A. Nursing home in the mid 1960's.

Turn right along Carmel Manor Drive and cut through the small parking area that serves a group of shops on S. Ft. Thomas Ave. Turn right and follow this main route, northward, paralleling the western edge of the Reservation. The old **Armory**, now a component of Tower Park, houses basketball courts, a game room and community exercise facilities. Returning to the Park's entrance, your walking tour has totalled 1.4 miles.

*Homes along Alexander Circle
enjoy a spectacular view of the Ohio Valley*

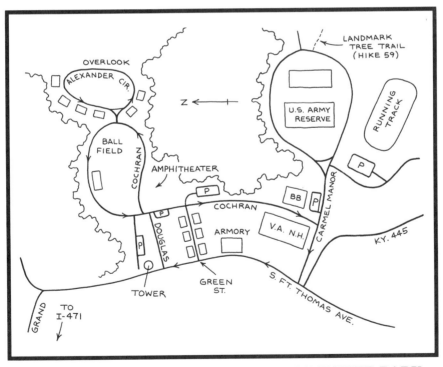

FT. THOMAS MILITARY RESERVATION/TOWER PARK

59 FORT THOMAS LANDMARK TREE TRAIL

Distance: 1.1 mile
Terrain: hilly

Under the leadership of Bill Thomas, the Fort Thomas Tree Commission has taken steps to protect the city's most secluded parcel of old-growth forest. Equipped with donated supplies and an army of volunteers, Thomas supervised construction of the **Landmark Tree Trail** during the winter and spring of 1993.

The 1.1 mile trail winds across a forested slope of the Ohio River Valley, dropping up to 200 feet from the trailhead on Carmel Manor Drive. Access to this secluded woodland was granted by the Carmel Manor Nursing Home, which owns most of the property, and by Mr. Ed Wilbers; the city of Fort Thomas has leased the trail right-of-way from these private land holders. Visitors should respect this arrangement by staying on the trail at all times.

A trail guide, available at the trailhead, describes fifteen numbered trees that will be encountered along the route. Fourteen of these trees are estimated to be at least 125 years old. These old giants are immersed in a rich deciduous forest, dominated by maple, beech and buckeye trees. Colorful redbuds and numerous wildflowers adorn the forest in spring and birdwatching can be excellent along the winding trail.

Directions:

From Cincinnati, cross the Ohio River on I-471 and continue southward. Take the Grand Avenue/Ky 1892 Exit (Exit #3) and turn left, following Grand Avenue as it winds up the Fort Thomas ridge. Drive 1.7 miles and turn right on S. Fort Thomas Ave. Pass Tower Park and the Fort Thomas Military Reservation, on your left, and turn left on Carmel Manor Drive. Park at the running track or near the trailhead, which is just behind the U.S. Army Reserve Center; **do not** park at Carmel Manor Nursing Home. The Trail is for hikers only; bikes are **not** permitted.

Route:

The **Landmark Tree Trail** begins on the southeast side of Carmel Manor Drive, just before the Nursing Home entrance. As noted above, trail guides are available at the trailhead; please return them after your hike.

The trail enters the forest, merges with a path from the Carmel Manor driveway and soon forks at **Tree #1**, a 40 year old Kentucky Coffeetree; though not as old as the forest giants, this specimen was featured since it is the State Tree of Kentucky. Continue straight ahead to **trees #2 and #3**, old Shumard Oaks. Across from Tree #3 a side path leads out to ruins from the old Fort Thomas military fort (see map).

Return to the main trail, descending past **Tree #4**, a 175 year old Northern Red Oak and cross a stream. The trail now climbs onto **"Riverview Ridge,"** which offers a broad view of the Ohio River Valley during the "leafless" months of fall, winter and early spring. **Tree #5**, another Old Northern Red Oak, stands near the crest of the ridge.

Curving northward, the trail descends toward its lowest point. **Tree #6**, a 225 year old Sycamore, has a circumference of 14 feet, largest of any tree in the preserve. The oldest (350 years) tree in the forest is a Chinkapin Oak, **Tree #7**. At **Tree #8**, a 140 year old White Ash, the Landmark Tree Trail curves back to the south where **Tree #9**, an old Northern Red Oak, has been used as a nest site by red-tailed hawks. The Trail recrosses the creek via a fine wooden bridge and curves westward,

A sunny day on Riverview Ridge

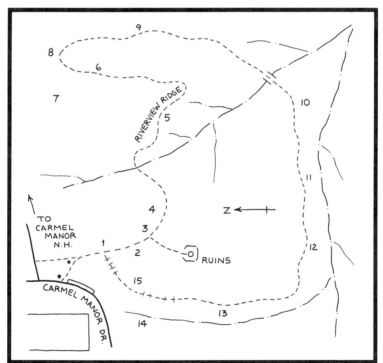

THE LANDMARK TREE TRAIL

gradually climbing along another stream. **Tree #10** is a 200 year old Northern Red Oak while **Trees #11-14** are all Shumard Oaks.

Leaving the main creek, the trail turns northward for a steep ascent along a tributary. **Tree #15**, a 175 year old Chinkapin Oak, signals the end of your loop hike. Turn left on the entry trail and exit the forest.

APPENDIX I

A Brief History of Greater Cincinnati

A commitment to conservation is almost always rooted in a knowledge of history. Those dedicated to the protection of natural habitat and endangered species have some understanding of natural history, including the phenomena of evolution, natural selection, habitat destruction and extinction. In a similar vein, historic preservationists have an appreciation for the commercial, cultural and architectural heritage of our cities and how it has been impacted by the forces of "development and modernization."

To augment your knowledge of Cincinnati's prehistoric and historic past, and to thereby encourage your commitment to conserving her natural and cultural heritage, we present the following chronology of events.

PRECAMBRIAN ERA (4600 to 600 MYA*)

The first 4 billion years of earth history were characterized by cooling of the planet's crust, evolution of the atmosphere and formation of the primordial oceans. Life evolved in the sea about 3.6 billion years ago, protected from intense solar radiation by the nourishing ocean waters. By the end of the era a remarkable diversity of primitive marine invertebrates had evolved.

PALEOZOIC ERA (600 to 225 MYA)

Shallow seas bathed large portions of our continent during the Paleozoic Era, depositing the shales, limestones, sandstones and other sedimentary rocks that we find today. **Ordovician** seas covered Greater Cincinnati 500 million years ago, depositing shales and limestones that harbor the fossils of primitive marine invertebrates. Explore any creek bed or road cut in the region and you will find these rocks, including their fossilized cargo of trilobites, bryozoans and brachiopods. An upward "bowing" of the deeper Precambrian rocks, known as the "Cincinnati Arch," kept these Ordovician sediments above the level of late Paleozoic and Mesozoic seas which deposited younger rocks across most of our continent.

Plants first colonized the land during the **Silurian Period,** 440 to 400 million years ago, when atmospheric oxygen had increased sufficiently to create the ozone layer, a protective blanket against the sun's ultraviolet radiation. Amphibians, which first appeared in the **Devonian Period (400-350 MYA),** reached giant proportions during the **Carboniferous Period (350-270 MYA)** when vast swamplands of giant horsetails and tree-sized ferns covered much of the continent; these swamp plants would later produce the rich coal seams of the Appalachian belt.

At the end of the Paleozoic Era, during the **Permian Period,** earth's continents merged into the giant land mass of Pangea. It was during this congregation that the North American and African plates collided, pushing up the Appalachian Mountains.

*MYA - million years ago

MESOZOIC ERA (225 to 65 MYA)

Most of earth's land mass was aligned along the equator during the early Mesozoic, producing a hot, dry climate and setting the stage for the rise of the dinosaurs. Crocodiles, turtles and small, herbivorous dinosaurs appeared during the **Triassic Period (225-190 MYA)**.

Early in the **Jurassic Period (190-135 MYA)**, Pangea split into Laurasia (the northern continents) and Gondwanaland (the southern continents). Large dinosaurs, including allosaurus and stegosaurus appeared, conifers reached their evolutionary peak and flowering plants first colonized the globe. By the end of the period, small, shrew-like creatures had evolved--the first primitive mammals.

During the **Cretaceous Period (135-65 MYA)**, dinosaurs reached their evolutionary peak, heralded by the reign of Tyrannosaurus rex. Marsupials evolved in Gondwanaland while the ancestral eutherians (placental mammals) spread across Laurasia.

Though dinosaurs once roamed across Greater Cincinnati, conditions did not favor their fossilization in our region. Rather, dinosaur fossils abound in areas where shallow Mesozoic seas and riverbeds encased these creatures in sediment soon after their death. The Mesozoic sandstones of the Rocky Mountain region and Colorado Plateau are the mecca for American paleontologists. Dinosaurs that lived and died in other parts of our continent, including Greater Cincinnati, did not leave behind a fossil record; their carcasses, left unprotected, were consumed by other creatures and degraded by the forces of erosion.

CENOZOIC ERA (65 MYA to Present)

The onset of the Cenozoic Era was marked by a cooling of earth's climate and the demise of the dinosaurs. The Rocky Mountains pushed skyward early in the Era setting the stage for the evolution of the Great Plains. Cut off from Pacific moisture by the Rocky Mountain chain and subjected to periods of drought, the central longitudes of North America witnessed the birth of prairie grasslands. These nutritious plains favored the evolution of large mammals (horses, rhinoceros, camels) which relied on speed and herding behavior to evade primitive carnivores.

Periods of glaciation occured throughout the Cenozoic, "tying up" vast quantities of water in the glacial ice and thereby lowering the level of earth's oceans. As sea level fell, land bridges opened between the continents, permitting the migration of mammals. Primitive bison, deer, mastodons and mammoths crossed into North America from Asia while horses, camels and rhinoceros moved the opposite direction.

Glacial activity reached its peak during the **Pleistocene Epoch**, commonly known as the "Ice Age." Beginning 2 million years ago, the Epoch was characterized by four major glacial advances, separated by relatively warm interglacial periods. The second ice advance, the **Kansan Glacier,** plowed deep into western Ohio and eastern Indiana approximately 1.2 million years ago. This massive ice sheet, up to a mile thick, blocked the course of the **Teays River** which originated in the Virginia Appalachians and flowed northwestward through West Virginia, Ohio and Indiana. Diverted to the south, this ancient river system gave rise to the **Ohio River** and its many tributaries. Outwash from the Kansan Glacier compacted into "conglomerate rock" which is now exposed along steep slopes of the central Ohio Valley (see Boone County Cliffs hike).

The most recent glacial advance was the **Wisconsin Ice Sheet** which plowed southward across today's "Corn Belt" approximately 70,000 years ago. The Wisconsin Glacier scooped out the Great Lake basins and enriched Midwestern States with glacial till, a fertile medium for the tallgrass prairie. Retreating into Canada 15-10,000 years ago, the ice sheet left erratic boulders, kettle lakes and altered landscape across the region.

Contrary to popular images, the earth was not "locked in ice" during the Pleistocene. Relatively minor cooling of the planet's climate initiated the glacial advances, as increased winter snows and shortened summer melting led to buildup of ice at the poles and atop the mountain ranges. Infact, many climatologists believe that we are currently in another interglacial period and that the "ice" will return within 10-50,000 years.

Man evolved in East Africa during the latter half of the Pleistocene and, by the end of the Epoch, his influence was felt across all continents except Antarctica. The first humans to reach the Americas arrived via "Beringea," a land bridge connecting Asia and Alaska which was uncovered as sea levels fell during the Wisconsin Glaciation. These first Americans, dominated by nomadic bands of hunters, followed the great herds of mammoth and bison and were likely south of the Glacier by 15-20,000 years ago.

With the onset of the **Holocene Period (10,000 years ago to the present),** the earth's climate was warming, the Wisconsin glacier had retreated and native Americans had adopted an "Archaic" lifestyle, with relatively permanent settlements. Among the early Ohioans were the Adena and Hopewell cultures, known as the "mound builders," who occupied the Ohio Valley some 2000 years ago. Their ceremonial earthworks are still found across southern Ohio today (see Shawnee Lookout Park). Modern Indian tribes, including the Shawnee, Miami and Delaware Indians, settled across the Ohio Valley during the 17th Century.

Recorded history of the Greater Cincinnati region began when the first white explorers and trappers crossed the Appalachians. Below is a chronology of regional history, focusing on persons and events covered in this guide.

1788 - Major Benjamin Stites and cohorts found the town of Columbia at "Turkey Bottoms," the present-day site of Lunken Airport
 - The town of Losantiville is established at Yeatman's Cove, across from the mouth of the Licking River
1789 - John Cleves Symmes founds the village of North Bend
 - Fort Washington is established at the edge of Losantiville
 - Covalt Station is built at present-day Terrace Park
1790 - Losantiville is renamed "Cincinnati" by Arthur St. Clair, Governor of the Northwest Territory
 - The first Protestant Church in the Northwest Territory is founded at Columbia
1795 - Newport, Kentucky, is founded by General James Taylor and his wife, Keturah Moss Leach
 - McFarland Station is constructed at present-day Pleasant Ridge
 - Montgomery, Ohio, is settled
1796 - Milford, Ohio, is established along the Little Miami River
1799 - The Newport Academy opens, becoming only the second educational institution west of the Appalachians

1802 - William McMillan founds "Home Plantation" which will later become Avondale
- Montgomery, Ohio, is platted
1804 - Newport Barracks begins operations at the confluence of the Licking and Ohio Rivers
1811 - The first steamship to reach Cincinnati, The Orleans from Pittsburgh, docks at the Public Landing
1815 - Covington, Kentucky, is platted
1817 - Piatt Park is donated to Cincinnati by John and Benjamin Piatt
1819 - The University of Cincinnati is founded
1820 - The Martin Baum House is built (now the Taft Museum)
1822 - Construction of Mariemont begins
1825 - William Henry Harrison is elected to the Senate
1827 - The Cincinnati-Dayton portion of the Miami-Erie Canal opens
1831 - Xavier University is founded (originally called the Athenaeum)
- Woodward High School opens, the first public high school west of the Appalachians
1835 - Covington is incorporated
1836 - Milford is incorporated
1840 - The peak decade of the Riverboat Era is beginning
- The Little Miami Railroad is constructed
1841 - William Henry Harrison is inaugurated President of the United States; he dies one month later, the first U.S. President to die while in office
1843 - Cincinnati's first Observatory is dedicated on Mt. Ida at the present-day site of the Holy Cross Monastery; Mt. Ida is renamed Mt. Adams to honor President John Quincy Adams
1845 - Spring Grove Cemetery is established
-. St. Peter in Chains Cathedral is completed
1849 - "Home City," the forerunner of Sayler Park, is founded
1850 - Clifton is incorporated
1852 - Good Samaritan Hospital is founded by the Sisters of Charity
1853 - Avondale is incorporated
1855 - Glendale is incorporated
1859 - Eden Park is established
1861 - Wyoming, Ohio, is founded by Robert Reily
1862 - The Church of the Immaculate Conception is dedicated on Mt. Adams
1866 - Bellevue, Kentucky, is founded by Albert S. Berry
- The Plum Street Temple is built
1867 - The Public Library of Cincinnati and Hamilton County is established
- The John A. Roebling Suspension Bridge opens
1869 - Highland Cemetery is dedicated
- The Cincinnati Art Academy is founded
- The Cincinnati Red Stockings become the first professional baseball team
1870 - Bellevue, Kentucky, is incorporated
1871 - The Mother of God Church is dedicated in Covington
- The Tyler Davidson Fountain is dedicated in downtown Cincinnati
1872 - Burnet Woods is set aside as parkland
1873 - The first May Festival is held (the oldest annual choral festival in the Americas)

1875 - The Cincinnati Observatory moves to Mt. Lookout
     - Hebrew Union College is founded by Dr. Isaac M. Wise
     - The Cincinnati Zoological Garden opens
1878 - Music Hall opens to the public
     - The Cincinnati, Georgetown & Portsmouth Railroad begins operation
1884 - The Campbell County Courthouse is completed
1887 - The Cincinnati Art Academy moves to Eden Park
     - The Fort Thomas Military Reservation is established
1888 - Fernbank, Ohio, is incorporated; it will later become part of Sayler Park
1891 - Pleasant Ridge is incorporated
1892 - The Cincinnati City Hall Building is completed
1893 - Terrace Park is incorporated
1894 - The Eden Park Water Tower is constructed
1895 - The Cincinnati Country Club is established (the oldest golf club west of
       the Appalachians)
     - The University of Cincinnati moves to its Clifton campus
1896 - Hyde Park is incorporated
1899 - Holy Cross Monastery is completed on Mt. Adams
1901 - Cathedral Basilica of the Assumption is dedicated in Covington
1902 - Our Lady of Providence Academy opens in Newport
1905 - Lytle Park is purchased by the city of Cincinnati
     - The Eden Park Spring-House gazebo is built
1908 - Mt. Echo Park is established
1910 - Queen City Beach, in Bellevue, Kentucky, gains National reputation as a
       fabulous inland resort
     - Montgomery is incorporated
     - Devou Park is donated to the city of Covington
1911 - Mt. Storm Park is purchased by Cincinnati
     - Home City is annexed by Cincinnati and is renamed Sayler Park
1912 - The Fitzhugh Thornton Memorial is dedicated in Sayler Park
1914 - Fort Thomas, Kentucky, is incorporated
     - Caldwell Park is donated to the city of Cincinnati
1915 - Good Samaritan Hospital moves to Clifton
1916 - Alms Park is donated to the city of Cincinnati
1919 - Xavier University moves to its Avondale campus
     - Withrow High School opens as East Side High
1920 - Work begins on the ill-fated Cincinnati Subway System
1926 - Central Parkway is completed
1930 - The Carew Tower is completed
1932 - Plantings begin at the Mt. Airy Arboretum
     - Lunken Airport opens, becoming the largest municipal airport in the
       U.S.
     - Sharon Woods becomes the first Hamilton County Park
     - The Taft Museum is donated to Cincinnati by Charles P. Taft
1937 - The Great Flood occures; its impact was worsened by construction of
       dams, locks and levees along the Ohio
     - The Stephen Foster Memorial is dedicated in Alms Park
     - California Woods Nature Preserve is established
1939 - Winton Woods becomes the second member of the Hamilton County
       Park District

1940 - Stanbery Park and Fairview Park are deeded to the Cincinnati Park Board

1945 - LaBoiteaux Woods is donated to the city of Cincinnati

1947 - The Delta Queen, built in California in 1926, adopts Cincinnati as its home port

1956 - The Arboretum Center is constructed at Mt. Airy Forest

1960 - The Playhouse in the Park opens
- The Nature Center building is completed at LaBoiteaux Woods

1964 - The Miami Purchase Association (now the Cincinnati Preservation Association) is founded

1967 - The Cincinnati Nature Center is established
- Shawnee Lookout Park is dedicated
- The Cincinnati Convention Center opens

1970 - Riverfront Stadium opens
- Avon Woods Outdoor Education Center is established by the Cincinnati Recreation Commission

1972 - Tower Park, in Fort Thomas, is dedicated
- Farbach Werner Nature Preserve is added to the Hamilton County Park District
- The initial section of the downtown Skywalk opens

1975 - Riverfront Coliseum is completed

1976 - The Ray Abercrombie Trail is dedicated at Caldwell Park
- Yeatman's Cove Park opens on the Cincinnati Riverfront

1978 - The MainStrasse Village Association is founded in Covington

1980 - Woodland Mound Park is dedicated

1982 - Embshoff Woods joins the Hamilton County Park District

1983 - Withrow Nature Preserve is added to the Hamilton County Park District

1984 - The Vietnam Memorial is dedicated in Eden Park

1985 - Oxbow, Inc., is founded to protect wildlife habitat across the floodplain of the Great Miami River

1987 - The expanded Convention Center reopens in downtown Cincinnati and is renamed to honor Dr. Albert Sabin

1988 - BiCentennial Commons at Sawyer Point is dedicated
- The Historic Figure bronze statues are dedicated in Covington's Riverside Historic District

1989 - Watertown Yacht Club opens in Dayton, Kentucky
- The Fairfield Avenue Historic district is dedicated in Bellevue, Kentucky

1990 - Work begins on the trail system through Highland Cemetery's forest preserve

1992 - The trail system at Seymour Nature Preserve is improved
- The Magrish Riverlands Preserve is established at the mouth of the Little Miami River

1993 - The Fort Thomas Landmark Tree Trail is constructed

APPENDIX II

LOCAL CONSERVATION AND
PRESERVATION ORGANIZATIONS

Audubon Society of Ohio
4945 Tealtown Road
Milford, Ohio 45150
576-0305

Bellevue Historic Preservation Commission
616 Poplar St.
Bellevue, Kentucky 41073
431-8866

Cincinnati Historical Society
1301 Western Ave.
Cincinnati, Ohio 45203
287-7032

Cincinnati Museum of Natural History
1301 Western Ave.
Cincinnati, Ohio 45203
287-7000

Cincinnati Nature Center
4949 Tealtown Road
Milford, Ohio 45150
831-1711

Cincinnati Park Board
950 Eden Park Drive
Cincinnati, Ohio 45202
352-4080

Cincinnati Preservation Association
Hamilton County Memorial Building
1225 Elm St.
Cincinnati, Ohio 45210
721-4506

Cincinnati Recreation Commission
Two Centennial Plaza
805 Central Ave.
Cincinnati, Ohio 45202
352-4000

Cincinnati Wildflower Preservation Society/Southwest Chapter, Ohio Native Plant Society
338 Compton Road
Wyoming, Ohio 45215

Friends of Cincinnati Parks, Inc.
Two Centennial Plaza
805 Central Ave.
Cincinnati, Ohio 45202

Glendale Heritage Preservation
Glendale, Ohio 45246

Hamilton County Park District
10245 Winton Road
Cincinnati, Ohio 45231
East District Naturalist 563-4513
West District Naturalist 385-4811
Seasongood Nature Center 474-0580
Miami Whitewater Forest Center 367-4774
Agricultural Education Facility 521-3276

Hillside Trust
3012 Section Road, at French Park
Cincinnati, Ohio 45237
531-6334

Historic Conservation Office
Cincinnati Planning Department
Room 228, City Hall
801 Plum St.
Cincinnati, Ohio 45202
352-3263

Historic Preservation Office
Economic Development Department
638 Madison Ave.
Covington, Kentucky 41011
292-2111

Little Miami, Inc.
3012 Section Road, at French Park
Cincinnati, Ohio 45237
351-6400

MainStrasse Village Association
616 Main St.
Covington, Kentucky 41011
491-0458

Milford Historical Society
Promont
906 Main St.
Milford, Ohio 45150
248-0324

Montgomery Historical Society
7650 Cooper Road
Montgomery, Ohio 45242
891-2421

National Register of Historic Places
National Park Service
U.S. Department of the Interior
Washington, D.C. 20240

The Nature Conservancy
Kentucky Chapter
642 W. Main St.
Lexington, Kentucky 40508
606-259-9655

The Nature Conservancy
Ohio Field Office
1504 W. First Ave.
Columbus, Ohio 43212
614-486-6789

Newport Historic Preservation Office
330 York St.
Newport, Kentucky 41071
292-3630

Ohio Department of Natural Resources
Division of Natural Areas & Preserves
Fountain Square, Building F
Columbus, Ohio 43224
614-265-6453

Oxbow, Inc.
P.O. Box 43391
Cincinnati, Ohio 45243

Rivers Unlimited
3012 Section Road, at French Park
Cincinnati, Ohio 45237
351-4417

Sierra Club
Miami Group, Ohio Chapter
3012 Section Road
Cincinnati, Ohio 45237
841-0111

Wyoming Historical Preservation Commission
Wyoming, Ohio 45215

BIBLIOGRAPHY

1. Arcilesi, Leonard, "**A Historical Sketch of Hughes High School,**" Cincinnati, Ohio

2. Beasley, David, "**Happy Birthday MainStrasse!**" Tristate Magazine, Cincinnati Enquirer, 9/4/88

3. "**Bellevue Historic Survey,**" City of Bellevue, Kentucky

4. "**Bellevue, Kentucky, from Past to Present,**" Bellevue Centennial Booklet, 1970

5. **Bicentennial Flashback Series,** The Cincinnati Enquirer, 1988

6. "**The Bicentennial Riverwalk,**" Greater Cincinnati Bicentennial Commission, 1988

7. Brady, Lilia, "**A Walk Through History,**" Cincinnati Magazine, May, 1988

8. "**Brief History of Memorial Hall,**" The Miami Purchase Association, Cincinnati, Ohio, June, 1988

9. **Caldwell Park Trail Map,** Cincinnati Park Board

10. **California Woods Nature Preserve Trail Map,** Cincinnati Recreation Commission

11. **Cincinnati, A Guide to the Queen City and Its Neighborhods,** Writers' Program, Ohio, American Guide Series, 1943, sponsored by City of Cincinnati

12. "**Cincinnati Centerpiece,**" Progressive Architecture, October, 1985

13. **Cincinnati Nature Center Trail Map,** Cincinnati Nature Center, Milford, Ohio

14. DeBrosse, Jim, "**Landmarks: 2088, What Should Our City Save for the Future?**" Cincinnati Enquirer, 10/21/88

15. "**The Early History of Clifton, (from Nellie Brown's Scrapbook)**" Courtesy Cincinnati Preservation Association

16. "**East Newport Historic Homes Tour,**" Mansion Hill & Gateway Neighborhoods

17. "**East Row Historic District,**" Newport Historic Preservation Commission

18. **Evergreen Magazine,** Hamilton County Park District, Jim Rahtz, Editor, Cincinnati, Ohio

19. "**Exhibit: A Tour of Cincinnati Firehouse History,**" Datebook, Cincinnati Enquirer, Mary Napier, Editor, 12/18/88

20. Feck Luke, **Yesterday's Cincinnati,** Writers' Digest Books, F&W Publications, Inc., Cincinnati, 1975, 1987

21. **Glendale's Heritage,** Glendale Heritage Preservation, Glendale, Ohio, 1976

22. Green, Richard, "**Landmark Getting Facelift, Doctors Building to the Presidential Plaza,**" Cincinnati Enquirer, November 27, 1988

23. **Hamilton County Park District Nature Trail Guides,** 10245 Winton Rd., Cincinnati, Ohio 45231

24. Harmon, Frances, "**History Quiz**" (Old Woodward High Building), Tristate Magazine, Cincinnati, Enquirer, 8/21/88

25. **"Historic Newport,"** Kentucky Department of Travel Department

26. **"Historic Walking Tour, Wyoming, Ohio,"** Wyoming Historical Preservation Commission, April, 1988

27. Hume, Paul, **"Cincinnati: New Music Complex, U.S. Premiere,"** Washington Post, 4/15/72 (entered into Congressional Record of 4/18/72)

28. Kayser, Pat, **Cincinnati Without Fears or Tears, Indispensable Guide to Cincinnati,** Bicentennial Edition, Pat Kayser Books, Inc., Cincinnati, 1988

29. **"Landmarks of Historic Montgomery, A Walking Tour,"** Montgomery Landmarks Commission, Montgomery, Ohio, October, 1983

30. Langsam, Walter C. and Julianne Warren, **Cincinnati in Color,** Hastings House Publishers, New York, 1978

31. Linden-Ward, Blanche, **"Spring Grove Cemetery, A Self-Guided Walking Tour,"** Center of Neighborhood and Community Studies, University of Cincinnati, 1985

32. **"Little Miami Scenic River Basin Trail,"** Loveland Chamber of Commerce, Loveland, Ohio

33. **"The Little Miami State and National Scenic River,"** Ohio's Scenic Rivers, Division of Natural Areas and Preserves, Ohio Department of Natural Resources, Columbus, Ohio

34. Maslowski, Karl, **"An Old Path Becomes A New Trail,"** Naturalist Afield, Tristate Magazine, Cincinnati Enquirer, 10/30/88

35. **"Milford, Ohio. A Walking Tour of Old Milford"** The Milford Historical Society

36. **"Milford. A Pleasant Blend of Tradition & Progress"** Milford Area Chamber of Commerce

37. **"Mt. Airy Arboretum Guide,"** Cincinnati Board of Park Commissioners

38. **Mt. Airy Forest Map,** Board of Park Commissioners, City of Cincinnati, revised 6/4/81

39. **National Register of Historic Places,** National Park Service, U.S. Department of Interior, Washington, D.C.

40. **"Northern Kentucky Historic Back Roads Tour,"** by the Behringer-Crawford Museum

41. **Ohio Almanac 1970,** The Lorain Journal Company, Lorain, Ohio

42. **"The Renton K. Brodie Science & Engineering Complex,"** The Flow Sheet, Department of Chemical & Metallurgical Engineering, University of Cincinnati, February, 1968

43. Ruehrwein, Dick, Pam Folsom and Elizabeth Lampe, **Discover Newport, A Book for Children,** Creative Company, Cincinnati, 1990

44. Steinfirst, Donald, **"Cincinnati Opens New Concert Auditorium,"** Pittsburgh Post-Gazette, 12/4/67

45. Strebel Hartman, Margaret, **"A Walking Tour of Newport,"** 1974

46. Sweeney, Bobbie, **"What makes Ridge so pleasant?"** Suburban Life, January 7, 1976

47. **"Walking Tour of the Licking Riverside Historic District,"** Licking Riverside Civic Association, Covington, Kentucky

48. Wetenkanmp, Elmer, **"Bicentennial Commons Guide,"** Cincinnati Enquirer, Tempo Section, 6/2/88

49. **Xavier University Admissions Manual,** Xavier University, Cincinnati, Ohio 1988

Index

About the Authors:

Darcy & Robert Folzenlogen are physicians and outdoor enthusiasts. They have written and published a variety of regional guides, including those listed above. All of their books are dedicated to the themes of open space protection, wildlife conservation and historic preservation.